Communication Skills for Couples:

21 Practices: Work with your Partner to Build a Mindful Relationship, Improve Emotional Intelligence and Grow Empathy for Each Other (7 Day Challenge Inside)

Table of Contents

Introduction

Congratulations on downloading this book and thank you for doing so.

Healthy, happy relationships and happy endings are not something that's reserved only for the movies. Relationships are challenging, they are hard work and sometimes it may feel like a struggle to even try to understand your other half. But couples who love each other are committed to one thing - *putting in the effort to constantly improve the quality and happiness of their relationship.*

These couples have learned that being in a happy, healthy relationship is completely possible because they realize that effective communication skills are the key to deepening their bond and connection with each other. Couples who have been married for years use several communication skills to successfully understand each other.

The big question is, why do communication skills play such a profound and important role in the success of romantic relationships?

Communication is how couples express their love and emotion for each other. All those deep feelings of love that you feel inside you for your significant other, well, the only way they're going to know how you feel is through effective communication. It is more than just the verbal words that are uttered, it is about the nonverbal communication that takes place too. Since effective communication skills are the foundation upon which healthy, long-lasting romantic relationships are built, it is important for couples to master the 21-techniques needed to improve this aspect, which is what has brought you to this guidebook.

By the time you reach the end of this guidebook, you will be able to build a more mindful relationship, improve emotional intelligence, grow your empathy for each other and finally, improve your communication skills as a couple through the 7-day workshop exercises included in the final chapter.

There are plenty of books on this subject on the market, thanks again for choosing this one! Every effort was made to ensure it is full of as much useful information as possible, please enjoy!

Chapter 1: Skill #1 - Abandoning Your Ego

A loving relationship. That's what we all want. That's what we all desire.

But anyone who has ever been - or is currently- in a relationship will tell you that happy, loving, and healthy relationships are not something that happens just like that. It takes hard work and for both parties to be equally invested and committed enough to put in the effort to *want to build* this relationship.

According to psychologist K. Daniel O'Leary back in 2012 when he and his research team conducted a study into long-term marriages, what was interesting was that happy couples were the ones who both endorsed and expressed the positive feelings that they had for their partners or spouses. The study revealed that 40% of the couples who have been married for more than 10 years affirmed that they were still very much in love. How do they do it?

There's No Room for Ego in a Happy Relationship

The key findings of O'Leary's study were one very simple habit that these couples were doing - *they were focused on the positive feelings,* and they had no problem expressing or reaffirming these feelings about their partner. Positive feelings is the major difference, and therein lies the difference between couples who are happy long term, and couples who struggle to hold onto happiness and a lasting relationship.

An example of how negativity can affect your relationships is when we let ego and pride get in the way and cloud our judgment. Everyone has ego. We all have some level of ego and pride within us, and how clearly these traits get displayed depends on how well we can control them. The ego which is left unchecked can often cause tremendous havoc in a person's life, especially in the relationships which are closest to them. That's because ego is a negative emotion which causes feelings of resentment, anger, fear, and jealousy.

Ego can be a very powerful force that resides within all of us. The term egotistical love exists for a reason, and this isn't the good kind of relationship either. If we let our egos make the decisions instead of our hearts, that's where a lot of problems start to happen. When you let ego take the driver seat, it can cause you to manipulate your relationships, and be the main reason for a lot of arguments, fights, depressions, aggression, passive-aggressiveness, revenge, self-doubt, distrust, intolerance, blame, competition, putting down your partner, and even disrespectful gestures. All of these negative qualities will eventually cause your relationship to deteriorate and breakdown over time. It is an obstacle which prevents effective communication from taking place, and *that is why* it should have no room in your relationship from this point on.

Signs Your Ego Is Damaging Your Relationship

If you're wondering whether ego is playing a part in preventing effective communication from taking place with your partner, take a look at the following signs:

- You're constantly blaming your partner for everything, without taking any responsibility for your actions. It is always someone else's fault.

- You find yourself playing the "victim card" far too often in your relationship.

- You get jealous easily, which leads to a lot of arguments and blame. Jealousy tends to cause a lot of drama within your relationships and causing a lot of toxic energy to manifest itself.

- You fear being rejected by your partner, especially when they seem to be achieving more than you do.

- You feel the need to have the last word all the time, in every argument especially. It is always about you and your opinions, and you don't spend enough time thinking about how your partner feels or what they have to say.

Kicking Ego Out the Front Door Once and for All

If you're reading this book, then you know communication skills is something that you need to work on to improve your relationships. If ego has been a force that you've been dealing with until this point, then there's only one thing left for you to do - kick it out the front door where it belongs.

Ego does not belong in your relationship. It never has, and it never will. To get rid of ego once and for all and start improving communication between you and your significant other, the following strategies are something you need to start working on right now:

- **There's No Need to Always Be Right** - Sure, being right feels good, but you don't *always* have to be right all the time. It is okay to be wrong every now and again. Yes, it may be hard for you to do in the beginning, but this is something you *must* do if you want to start seeing any kind of improvement in your relationship. No one is perfect, and you shouldn't expect yourself to be perfect. There will be times when you find yourself in the wrong. Instead of becoming defensive, use these situations to learn from what went wrong.

- **You Don't Need to Be Superior -** Do you have this need to always be the one who's in charge? The one who's in control? Do you want to be better than everyone? That's ego at work there again. Instead of trying to compete to be better than everyone else all the time, especially your partner, why not focus on yourself and what *you can do to become a better person* overall? That would be the healthier approach not just for your relationships, but for your everyday life too.

- **Give Up Being Easily Offended -** If you find yourself getting offended far too easily, even over the simplest things, that's ego working behind the scenes again. People are not out to offend you on purpose, especially your partner, so it's time to start practicing a little bit more tolerance. Make it a conscious practice, and remind yourself that everyone expresses themselves differently. When you practice tolerance, it makes it easier to have effective conversations with your partner that don't escalate into arguments.

- **Be Forgiving -** Gandhi once said that "*forgiveness is something that is attributed to the strong*". He was right. Forgiveness is one of the most powerful tools you could possess to make letting go of your ego easier. Not only will you eventually gain the ability to forgive others over time when you let go of your ego, but you'll also learn to forgive yourself.

You'll learn acceptance, and you'll learn how to be much happier when you let go of all the anger that resides within you.

Chapter 2: Skill #2 - How to Build Healthy Habits as A Couple

How many times have you looked on with envy at other happy couples whom you know? Or even the happy couples that you randomly see around you gazing lovingly into each other's eyes or holding hands as they stroll through the park? They seem almost picture perfect, don't they? But of course, every relationship comes with its own challenges. These happy couples have just found a way to work through those challenges together by communicating well and relying on each other for support. That's the secret to their success.

Now, working on building a lasting relationship is not going to be easy. You can't just enter into a relationship and hope for the best - or that your problems are going to sort themselves out. In fact, the Public Discourse published an article in 2015 which revealed that at least 40-50% of marriages tend to end in divorce. Researchers who spend their time analyzing relationships have always been motivated to find the qualities and traits which contribute to the happiness of a relationship, and one of these factors is to start building happy relationships as a couple.

Healthy Habits That Happy Couples Engage In

Building a happy, healthy relationship starts with building healthy habits together as a couple. Which is why this is Skill #2 that you're about to learn. Why do we need to actively work on building healthy habits? Because in a 2013 *Journal of Social and Personal Relationships* publication by Ogolsky and Bowers, research supported the idea that those who put in the effort to work on their relationships were the ones who managed to cultivate relationships with lasting happiness.

There are healthy habits which happy couples regularly engage in, and here are some practices you can begin applying in your own relationship to improve how you communicate with your partner or spouse:

- **Always Express Your Appreciation -** Do it all day, every day because you can never express appreciation enough. It is always better that your partner feels the extra love and appreciation that you feel for them instead of feeling underappreciated. Love the little things that they do? Let them know! You don't have to do anything elaborate, just simple little gestures, thank you notes, even text messages sent throughout the day letting them know how much you appreciate them can make a huge difference in someone's day.

- **Ask, And You Shall Receive -** Another healthy habit that a lot of couples tend to ignore is to just ask for what they want. Don't assume your partner is going to pick up on the little hints or read your mind and know how to anticipate your thoughts. Assumption is where a lot of communication breakdown tends to happen, which then escalates into fights that could have been avoided. If you want your partner to do something, don't be afraid to just *ask* for it.

- **Working on Chores Together -** This is easily one habit that can be done together, so one person doesn't feel the burden of having to upkeep the house all by themselves. In fact, dividing the workload promotes great teamwork and a sense of happiness knowing that you can count on your partner to share in the workload with you. Rotate the chores amongst yourselves, so there's a sense of fairness and balance, and one person is not stuck doing the same thing all the time.

- **The Language of Love** - Gary Chapman is a relationship therapist who pioneered an excellent concept. This concept was called the Five Love Languages, which involved words of affirmation, physical touch, gifts, quality time and acts of service. This is an excellent habit for couples to start working on together, because the Five Love Languages teach you how to give and receive love with awareness, warmth, and love.

- **They Can Move On** - The biggest downfall in any relationship is the inability of one partner to let things go and move on. Sometimes perhaps both partners could have the tendency to hold onto grudges and bring up issues of the past in arguments. It is time to start cultivating the habit of letting this go. When you have a disagreement or an argument about something, work it out, apologize if need be, and then move on. Let that be the end of it. Forget about it and don't bring it up again in future arguments. It can be a difficult habit to start practicing and adopting in the beginning, but it is a habit that is going to make a huge difference in your relationship once you do.

- **Be Respectful Towards Each Other** - Couples that don't respect each other will have a much harder time staying together. Respect is a vital habit towards cultivating the happiness in your relationship that you seek. Each time that you show disrespect towards your partner, you are in a way letting them know that you don't accept them for the way that they are. Remember that your partner is a unique individual, just like you are, and part of being in a relationship is accepting others and valuing them for who they are, not who you expect them to be.

- **Indulge in Common Interests Activities -** Spend some time doing activities together that *both* you and your partner enjoy. There are bound to be some things that you have in common. It could be a hobby, sport or activity that you like to do together, a shared passion over food perhaps, or even a favorite TV show that both of you love. Make it a habit to do these things together as a couple, it can be great for enhancing your communication skills, especially for activities where you need to work together as a team.

- **Hugging Hello and Goodbye -** When you leave for work in the mornings, start making it a habit to hug your partner and tell them you love them before you head out the door (if you're not doing it already). Wish them a great day ahead, give them a kiss and a hug and those little habits can have a tremendous effect on how both of you feel. It's a great way to start the day on a positive note. When you come home from work in the evenings, greet each other again with a hug and a kiss, asking them how their day was and let them know that you missed them. You could even make this habit something that you do each time you leave or come home, even if it is for little things like running errands or going out to catch up with a few friends for a drink.

Chapter 3: Skill #3 - Developing Emotional Intelligence

Emotional intelligence may seem like it is a skill that better belongs in the workplace, but

Emotional intelligence - or EQ - is defined as an individual's capacity to control and regulate their emotions, and the emotions of others. These two traits are then used to better understand how to improve the interpersonal relationships that surround them, and perhaps even control and regulate the emotions of others to a certain extent.

EQ is a concept which was made popular by Daniel Goleman in his book of the same title, *Emotional Intelligence.* In his book, Goleman outlines just how EQ is growing in popularity as people all over the world are beginning to grasp just how important this quality is in contributing to their success. It doesn't matter if that success is in their career or their everyday life, because either way, EQ is going to provide everyone with the foundation that they need to start forging better, more meaningful connections and relationships. It is forging those deeper, more meaningful relationships that is going to be the exact reason why developing your EQ is going to be important for improving communication skills within your relationship.

In Goleman's book, he outlines the five main qualities (or core pillars as he calls them) that everyone with high EQ should possess - *self-awareness, self-regulation, social skills, motivation, and empathy.* To build effective, successful and meaningful relationships, you need to have mastered *all five* core pillars.

Signs That You or Your Partner May Be Lacking Emotional Intelligence

Because people with high levels of EQ have a much better grasp of their emotions and the way they regulate and control their responses, they tend to make much better partners or spouses. They don't fly off the handle for every little thing, they don't let their emotions dictate their actions and responses, and they have the ability to listen and empathize with others. All these qualities are what lead to better communication because it gives them the ability to remain calm in situations where someone with less EQ might completely overreact in ways that could make the situation worse.

There are several signs which might indicate that you (or your partner) may need to work on improving your EQ. The signs that you want to look out for are:

- **Poor Ability to Control Your Emotions -** If you find yourself losing your temper far too often, getting emotionally carried away in situations that have no real cause for it, you need to work on improving your EQ. Especially if you're guilty of the former, because anger can be an extremely disruptive force in any relationship which will cause it to eventually break down and deteriorate over time.

- **You Can't Read Emotions Properly -** A lack of self-awareness about the way others feel is also a sign of poor EQ. When you're unable to assess how the people around you feel, it becomes much harder for you to forge meaningful connections. Not only will you find it hard to relate to others, they too will find it hard to relate to you.

- **You Find It Hard to Maintain Relationships** - Not just romantic relationships, but any kind of relationships. Friendships, relationships with your family, colleagues, even your kids. Without the necessary social skills, empathy, and self-awareness, you're going to find it very hard to maintain any kind of lasting relationship in your life.

- **You Don't React Appropriately -** If you've ever witnessed someone overreacting or being too emotional and thought "well, that's a bit extreme", that's a sign that the person has poor EQ. They are not aware of their actions and they don't know how to regulate their behavior accordingly, which makes it very difficult for them to react the way that they should in any kind of social setting.

- **They Find It Hard to Cope -** Those with low EQ will find it very difficult to cope when any kind of emotion threatens to overwhelm them.

How to Work on Bettering Your Emotional Intelligence

Emotions are a large part of who we are as human beings. There's no escaping it or ignoring it, so why not learn to control it instead for our own benefit? If you've ever been so overwhelmed by your emotions that you reacted in a way which has caused you a lot of regrets later on, you'll understand just why it is so important to develop a high level of EQ.

We have all, at some point, said something out of anger or in the heat of the moment that we immediately regret as soon as the words have left our mouth, especially during arguments with our partner. While we may apologize profusely and sincerely later on, sometimes the hurt doesn't ever truly go away. Once something has been said, it cannot be taken back, no matter how much you want it to be.

Therefore, it makes sense that if you want to work on improving your relationship, especially the communication aspect of it, you need to first work on *your own emotions* and learn how to regulate your actions by working on improving your EQ. The good news is, anyone can develop a greater level of EQ over time and with a lot of practice:

- **You Need to Understand Yourself First -** Before you can begin to understand another, you must first work on developing a deeper understanding of *yourself*. Knowing who you are, why you react the way that you do is the key to begin developing a greater level of self-awareness. Take a step back and assess how you've been reacting to the different situations in your life and relationship this far and ask yourself, *why did I react that way?* Understand your emotional triggers, reflect on your actions, assess your emotions in detail, and do this as often as needed until you finally understand what makes you tick.

- **Naming Your Feelings -** Another great exercise which is going to enhance your self-awareness abilities is to name your feelings. Instead of just generalizing by saying *I am feeling happy,* define that emotion in greater detail. What level of happiness are you feeling? Cheerful? Joyful? Jubilant? Ecstatic? Practice this method, especially during the moments when you're experiencing those emotions intensely. Make a note of what triggered that reaction within you and then take a step back, assess the way you reacted at that moment and think about how you might have reacted better in such a situation.

- **Start Making Empathy a Habit -** It takes two people to make a relationship work, and your partner's feelings and emotions matter just as much as yours do. Being emotionally intelligent means you have to start developing the ability to empathize, to be able to put yourself in your partner's shoes and see things from their perspective. Being able to understand where they're coming from, feeling what they feel, is going to give you a greater ability to connect with them on a much deeper level than you were previously able to do. That is going to do wonders for improving the communication that occurs in your relationship because you're finally able to see things from your partner's point of view.

- **Knowing When to Walk Away -** An emotionally intelligent person will remain calm and collected. They know when to take a time out, and come back to the situation with a better solution. It is easy to let your feelings overwhelm you if you're not careful. As much as you want to resolve a conflict there and then, sometimes the best decision is to just walk away from the situation to clear your head whenever your emotions are starting to get the best of you. That is the intelligent thing to do, and when you're ready and much calmer, come back and revisit the situation again and see how you can resolve it much better this time.

Chapter 4: Skill #4 - Developing Empathy Listening

Well done on making it to skill #4! Hopefully, you've been practicing everything that was learned so far up to this point. Once you have successfully improved your EQ levels, you are now ready to dive a little deeper into the *empathy* portion of it by developing your empathic listening skills.

What Is Empathy Listening?

Essentially, empathy listening involves your ability to *genuinely listen* to what your partner is telling you. You listen sincerely with respect and understanding towards their ideas, values, and opinions. Being able to empathically listen allows you to be on the same page with them, and it is even going to help you on the emotional intelligence front when you need to start tapping into the empathy portion of it.

In a relationship, there is nothing more frustrating for your partner than to feel like they are not being heard. It works both ways too, because imagine if you were trying to express your needs and the way that you're feeling to your partner only to feel like they're not fully understanding what you're trying to communicate. You would feel frustrated too if you were put in that same spot.

Your partner needs to feel like they can come to you, open up and share their innermost feelings and have a conversation with you without the fear of being judged or ridiculed. They need to trust enough that their ideas and opinions are not going to be dismissed, or that you're not going to get defensive over something that's been said. In other words, empathy listening is creating that sense of security for your partner so that they know they can come to you about *anything* at all.

Why Empathy Listening Can Help Communication In a Relationship

Communication works both ways, and both people have to be equally invested in the conversation that's happening for the communication process to be considered effective. Empathy listening is going to be the skill that is going to help you bridge the gap and bring you even closer together with your partner. When they trust you enough and feel comfortable enough to have any kind of conversation with you, even the difficult ones, it can bring the two of you closer together.

Being an empathic listener for your partner doesn't mean that you necessarily have to agree with everything they are saying. Not at all. In fact, it is okay to have different opinions, but when empathy listening is involved, those difference of opinions have a much better chance of becoming healthy discussions rather than heated arguments. An example of when empathy listening is taking place is when you are able to respond *"I hear what you're saying and I understand why you feel that way, however...."* That's how a healthy discussion should be, and that's the kind of communication two people in a relationship should strive to achieve. If every couple practiced a little more empathy listening, there would be far less heated arguments in the world.

How to Develop Empathy Listening

We may not all be born with high levels of emotional intelligence, or a natural ability to be an empathic listener, but we *can learn to develop* these skills over time. And these are skills that you should work on developing too because they can lead to a much happier, more fulfilling life if everyone could have more empathy and try to connect better with the people around them. It isn't just going to help you in your romantic relationships, it is going to help you in *every* relationship you have in your life. When people start to see you as someone they can turn to, someone they can count on when they need someone to talk to, the connection between you and them starts to deepen and develop into something much more meaningful.

Developing your empathy listening skills is much easier than you think too.

- **It's About Them, Not You -** The first thing that you need to work on to start developing your empathy listening skills is to remember that it's *not about you, it's about them.* It is always about them when someone is trying to have a meaningful conversation with you. This is the time for you to put your needs above others. It can be a challenge to put your personal feelings and opinions aside for a few minutes but remind yourself that this is someone you love that's coming to talk to you. If you love them, then it's time to make it all about them for the next few minutes.

- **No Distractions -** The minute your partner comes to you and says they want to have a conversation, put away all distractions so you can focus on them for the next few minutes. Put your phone away, put your computer away, turn off the TV, anything that's going to pose a distraction, put it away. For the next few minutes, your only point of focus is going to be your partner and listening to what they need.

- **Listening Actively -** There's a very big difference between listening, and listening *actively*. You could be listening and nodding along, saying all the right things, but your mind is actually a million miles away or thinking about something else. That's not active listening. Active listening is when you take in everything that your partner is saving, process it and stay engaged throughout the entire conversation. You know exactly what to say, when to say it and how to say it because you have been paying attention. *That* is active listening.

- **Not Responding with Criticism -** With empathy listening, ideally you want to let your partner be the one who is doing all the talking. It is their time to talk. However, if they were to ask what you think or what you would suggest at some points during the conversation, then your job here is to not respond critically or judgmentally. Empathy listening is about making your partner feel supported, about letting them know that you can see things from their perspective, and you understand why they feel the way that they do. Don't ridicule, judge or criticize them for their opinions because remember, it is all about them this time.

- **Avoid Unsolicited Advice -** Sometimes your partner just needs you to listen to them and that is it. They need someone they can vent their feelings and frustrations to instead of keeping it bottled up inside. Your job, as the supportive partner, is to be what they need and avoid offering unsolicited advice. It can be very off-putting, even to your partner, when that happens, especially when you start telling them what you think they should, or should not do. Unless they specifically ask you for your opinion, remember that empathy listening is all you need to do right now.

Chapter 5: Skill #5 - Don't Be Afraid to Show Weakness

In a loving, healthy and happy relationship, you shouldn't have to hide who you are. You should feel so comfortable that you don't feel the need to pretend to be someone that you are not. That special connection between two people is what makes life meaningful. In fact, it is hardwired within our brains to *want* to have these connections with the people who are in our lives. Families, communities, friendships, work, romantic relationships, these connections are all forged because there is something within us that wants to feel that closeness to another human being.

Why Being Vulnerable Can be a Good Thing for Your Relationship

Putting on a brave face all the time can be exhausting, both mentally and physically. Somewhere along the way we live, we somehow developed the belief that showing our vulnerable side is perceived as a sign of weakness - that if we show our vulnerable side, people might take advantage of it or worse, we open ourselves up to being hurt. In an attempt to protect our fragile hearts and shield ourselves from hurt, we have become afraid to show any sign of weakness.

Unfortunately, while your intentions may be good, closing yourself off in this way can also prevent you from connecting with your partner on an intimate level. You need to show your vulnerable side because as terrifying and scary as it is, you *need to know* that you can count on your partner in the moments when you need it the most. Being in a relationship means pain is sometimes unavoidable, but closing this part of yourself off completely from your partner is not the way to deal with it either.

How to Work On Being Less Afraid

It's going to take a while for you to be comfortable showing weakness. It is never easy, to open yourself up to the possibility of being hurt, but if you want to improve communication with your partner - *to be able to have open and honest discussions* - you need to able to talk about anything.

To start accepting that it is okay to show weakness in front of your partner is a process that needs to be worked through in the following stages:

- **Stage 1: Why Are You Reluctant to Show Weakness?** - Have you ever stopped to ask yourself why you feel reluctant to show any sign of weakness? Why do you struggle to reveal the most difficult parts of yourself, and why do you hesitate to open up to your partner? You need to get down to the root cause about what makes this process so difficult for you before you can begin moving onto the second point below. Pinpointing the root cause of the problem is how you begin to understand yourself on a deeper level, and when you do, you can then slowly open up and explain to your partner just exactly how you feel because you have a much better understanding of yourself too.

- **Stage 2: Working Through Your Emotions -** Only when you have pinpointed the root cause of what makes it difficult for you to open up to your partner can you then begin sorting through your emotions. If you don't work through your own emotions first, you're going to find having difficult conversations with your partner even more of a challenge. You will always struggle to find the right words, and struggle to put your *feelings into words* because you can't manage to work through your own emotions, let alone someone else's.

- **Stage 3: Baby Steps -** Exposing your vulnerable side is going to be a challenge, especially if you (or your partner) has spent all the time trying to do the very opposite by shutting yourself off from these emotions. That's okay, you've already done good so far by first trying to pinpoint why you feel the way that you do, and then trying to work through your emotions. You don't have to rush through the entire process. In fact, taking baby steps is one of the best things you can do for yourself in this situation as you gradually start to get comfortable. You need to be able to trust that your partner is not going to hurt you, and that is going to take a lot of strength to do. If your partner is the one who is afraid to show weakness, help them work through these stages and do it together with them. Treat it like a trust-building exercise that the two of you can work through.

- **Stage 4: Practice Makes Perfect -** It may sound weird to have to "practice" being vulnerable, but this is going to help you learn to trust your partner over time. Take it slow, and maybe once a week, sit down with your partner and talk about one weakness that you would normally otherwise try to hide. Tell them how you feel, why you feel this way, and how they could support you in making you feel comfortable about expressing this weakness moving forward. Practicing being vulnerable is merely a simple exercise of being able to talk about what you perceive as a "weakness" and being able to answer honestly if your partner has any questions about it. Working through this stage together and communicating as a couple is a great way to strengthen your bond, especially when you see that your partner is going to support you through it.

- **Stage 5: Being Honest -** This is a very important stage. This is where you're going to have to fight all your natural instincts to hide your true emotions by responding with the usual *"I'm fine"* phrase. If you're not feeling fine, then tell your partner. Let them in instead of shutting them out. If there is something that they can do to help you feel better, to feel safer, to feel more accepted, let them know. Let them in on this journey with you, they can only help you and support you the way that you need if they can understand what you're going through.

- **Stage 6: Creating Your Safe Space -** Sometimes it helps to create a safe space where you can have these difficult and intimate discussions with your partner. Creating a safe space within your home, where the two of you can sit down and communicate about this is essential for creating the right frame of mind and the right environment for a conducive, healthy discussion. Talking about this in a situation where you or your partner might be distracted, agitated, anxious, or maybe even just not in a good mood at the moment is going to make it harder for a meaningful conversation to take place. You're opening up to your partner about the things that worry about the most, and this is a very important talk which must be done at the right time and in the right place.

Chapter 6: Skill #6 – Understanding Body Language

Did you know that 55% of our communication is demonstrated through our body language? This was certainly a very interesting revelation by the author of *Silent Messages*, Dr. Albert Mehrabian. According to Dr. Mehrabian, only 7% of our communication occurs through the use of words, and that, compared to body language, is a very small percentage. It, therefore, goes without saying that body language plays a very important, if not crucial role, in being able to effectively communicate in relationships.

If you are correctly able to read someone's body language, you've already got incredible leverage on your hands right now. It is this very skill that is going to help you deduce how a person truly feels without them having to ever say a word, especially if this person is your partner. By being able to read these signals, you'll be able to anticipate their needs much better and support them in ways they may not even realize that they want at the time. A lot of body language occurs on a subconscious level, without us even realizing it. Our words may say that we're fine, but our bodies are telling a completely different story altogether.

Basic Cues to Reading Your Partner's Body Language Correctly

In a relationship, your partner may be displaying a wide array of body language signals that signify what's on their mind or how they may be feeling at that time. Communicating effectively with your partner in any situation is going to depend heavily on your ability to read the signals that they are giving off, and better understand their moods so you will be able to adjust and moderate your responses and reaction to better suit the situation.

Body language can be complex, but at the same time, extremely fascinating. It is like unlocking clues to a puzzle, where the more you understand, the greater your awareness will be. In this case, the puzzle is your partner and what you're trying to do is understand how they feel without them having to tell you. Body language can give you clues into the feelings that they may not want to reveal, and when used correctly, can rapidly change the way that you and your partner communicate.

You don't have to be an expert to start picking up on the little body language nuances that your partner may be exhibiting. In fact, some clues are just a matter of paying attention and noticing the little things. That alone is going to make all the difference in the world in the way that you communicate and anticipate their needs.

- **Facial Expressions -** This is where most of the body language signals are going to emit from - the facial expressions. Anything from the eyes, the lips, mouth, or even the way that they tilt their head is going to mean something. If your partner lifts their eyebrows, for example, this could signal skepticism, surprise or discomfort. If their mouth and lips are pursed in a thin line, it could mean that they are unhappy, irritated or angry. The clenching of the jaw which might happen during an argument could signal to you that they are stressed or angry.

- **Eye Contact -** Another big one you want to look out for is eye contact. If, during a conversation, you notice that your partner's eyes are unfocused or looking behind you, for example, it could mean that they are preoccupied, distracted, anxious or maybe just not that interested in the conversation. Eye contact is another way of detecting when someone may or may not be telling the truth. According to several body language experts, whenever a person is telling a lie, they tend to look towards the left. They also struggle to maintain consistent eye contact the way a person would do if they were being honest. If you're trying to suss out whether your partner may be lying to you or not, look for these indicators and see how well they manage to maintain eye contact.

- **The Arms and the Hands -** The arms and hand gestures are a bit of a tricky one because they could hold several different meanings. Crossing arms in front of the chest, for example, doesn't necessarily mean that your partner is closed off to the conversation or shutting you out. They could be doing this out of habit, because it's a comfortable position, or maybe because they happen to feel cold. You'll need to observe the context in which this gesture is occurring. If your partner crosses their arms in front of their chest halfway during a disagreement, for example, it means they are being defensive. On the other hand, if you notice that your partner has their palms facing up and outwards during a conversation, this is a good sign because it means they are relaxed, honest and sincere. If your partner clenches their fists, it could be a signal that they're feeling angry or tense.

- **The Proximity -** How close someone chooses to be next to you is a signal about how they feel about you. If your partner chooses to stand close to you in a relaxed, comfortable manner, they are happy and comfortable being around you and being in your presence. If they move away from you however, it means the opposite.

- **Fidgeting About** - Any fidgeting, either while sitting, is a sign that your partner may be feeling irritated, bored or anxious. This is applicable too if they fiddle with their hands, or even objects in their hands. If you're about to have a serious conversation with them and you notice all these signs beforehand, you might want to think about postponing the talk to another time when they are much calmer. Ask them what's wrong when you see these signs at work and encourage them to talk about it, especially if they are feeling particularly nervous or anxious.

Other general signs of body language that you might often see happening in your relationship with your partner include:

- **Brow Rubbing:** An indication they could be worried or doubtful.

- **Head Scratching:** An indication they could be deep in thought or trying to solve a problem. Sometimes used to indicate confusion too.

- **Nose Touching:** Generally associated with being an indication that a person is lying. If casually done, it could be an indication that they may feel pressured about something.

- **Ear Rubbing:** Specifically, rubbing behind the ears. This is an indication your partner is afraid of being misunderstood, or they are afraid they're not going to understand.

- **Finger Pointing:** An indication that they could be feeling authoritative. Also sometimes an indication of aggressive or angry emotions.

How Does Your Partner Behave During an Argument?

During a disagreement, you may be so wrapped up in having your say and focused on your own feelings that you forget to think about how your partner feels in this situation. But paying attention to body language is exactly what you need to be thinking about too because reading the signs is exactly what's going to help you diffuse the situation much faster. When you notice the following signs which signal disapproval, feelings of aggression or anger, it's time to take a step back and start to approach the argument differently:

- Nostrils flared

- Teeth bared

- Sneering

- Arms crossed tightly in an angry manner across the chest

- Frown between the eyes

- The body turned to point away from you

- Pointing or jabbing you

- Clenched fists

- Invading your personal space

- Posture is stiff and rigid

- Contracted pupils

- Rapid body movements

- Rubbing the back of the neck

Chapter 7: Skill #7 – Learning to Talk About It

Having difficult conversations can be, well, difficult. Unfortunately, as much as we would like to avoid having these discussions, it is not always possible. In any relationship, there is going to come a time where you're going to have these difficult conversations, especially in a romantic relationship where you're sharing so much of your life with another individual.

Why You Need to Learn to Talk About It

Because you can't avoid problems and issues forever. There is no "wishing it would go away" or sweeping it under the rug and pretending like it doesn't exist. That's not a healthy relationship, and it won't be a recipe for a long-lasting relationship either. No, whether you like it or not, you need to learn to talk about it.

The more you ignore your problems, the harder they will be to fix. In a scenario where your partner may want to talk about and address these issues but you don't, it can cause a lot of frustration, tension, and resentment over time. Your partner will get frustrated eventually over your refusal to talk things about, and eventually, it will cause your relationship to break down, possibly even end, if your partner feels like they are getting nowhere with you.

Relationships are not easy, and conflict is something that comes along with the package. While conflict and the issues that arise are sometimes beyond your control, what you *do have control* over is how you handle and manage the situation.

Start Learning How to Talk About It

If you're worried that talking about it could lead to potential arguments, don't be. Just because it is a difficult conversation, it doesn't mean that there can only be one outcome - or that it has to end badly in a heated debate between you and your partner. You have the power to control your outcome when you learn how to talk about it by following these strategies:

- **Understand Your Why -** Before you even begin, it is important that you understand *why* you're learning to talk about things. You may not like it and you may not even want it, but this is something that you're going to have to do regardless. *Why?* Because that's what healthy relationships are about. It is not about living in denial, ignoring the problem and hoping it is going to resolve itself. No, to have a relationship that is both happy and healthy, you *must* be able to talk about anything, both good and bad.

- **Remaining Calm -** The ability to stay calm is going to be your biggest asset in determining a positive outcome for any conversation that you have, especially the difficult ones. This is where the emotional intelligence and empathy listening skill is going to be extremely beneficial to you. During a conversation that is particularly difficult, you can sometimes struggle to maintain your composure or to keep your voice calm and friendly. When your voice starts to escalate, your partner is likely going to follow because they will sense all that nervous and tense energy that is happening and find it hard to keep their emotions in check too. Whenever you feel yourself start to get more emotional, press pause on the conversation, explain to your partner why you're doing so, and then suggest that the two of you take a 10 to 15-minute break before revisiting this issue again when you're both much calmer.

- **Use Positive Language -** Learning to talk about the things that are difficult can be much easier if both you and your partner adopt the approach to only use positive language during the conversation. Phrases such as *I hear what you're saying and I value what you have to say* or *I know this is difficult to talk about, but I'm here to support you and we can work through this together* are examples of some great positive language that can be used to help control the conversation and steer it in the right direction. It minimizes the chances of things escalating and getting out of hand.

- **Stay Relevant -** Another important aspect of learning how to talk about difficult matters is to remember to remain relevant. Talk about the situation or issue that is currently happening, and avoid bringing up past arguments to support your case. This will only serve to either hurt your partner's feelings by reminding them that you haven't forgotten or let go of what's happened in the past, or it could make them defensive and shut them off to the conversation completely. There is no need to rehash old arguments, in fact, Skill #1 is what you need to bring into play right now and abandon your ego. Leave it outside where it belongs.

- **Manage Your Expectations -** If you start a conversation with your partner with a mindset that this is going to go badly, then that's all you're going to be thinking about and guess what? You'll probably sabotage the conversation and make it worse without even realizing it. Why? Because you *expected it.* Learning to talk about difficult topics with your partner can be hard, but going into it with a negative mindset is only going to make it harder for both of you to achieve a fruitful discussion. Instead, keep an open mind about it. You might just be surprised at the outcome.

- **Pick the Right Time -** With difficult conversations, timing is everything. You need to pick the right time, place and be in the right frame of mind to have this conversation. Not just you, but your partner too. The best time to talk about what you and your partner may find difficult is when you're both feeling calm, relaxed and in an environment where the two of you feel safe and happy. It is best that the environment is free from distractions too, so both of you can focus on the conversation at hand. Choosing to talk about it when someone is doing the dishes, watching television, or just returned from a stressful day, for example, is *not the right time* to have a difficult conversation.

- **Be Respectful -** A lot of couples prefer not to talk about things because they don't want to risk an argument. In the heat of the moment, words get thrown out and often, these may be words that we later come to regret. It's perfectly understandable to feel this way, and what's going to help you during this situation is to remember to always be respectful towards your partner. After all, this is someone that you love, someone you care for deeply and you would never want to hurt them under any circumstances. Let your partner know before you begin that you're about to talk about something which you find difficult so that they are on board with what's happening.

Chapter 8: Skill #8 – Digitally Disconnecting

Does your partner complain that you're on the phone far too much? Or perhaps it happens far too often where you want some quality time with your partner, only to find that they're not 100% present with you because they're too preoccupied with scrolling through social media?

The digital world we live in today is great, but it has also created several problems in the process. One of these problems is interrupting quality time which could be invested in romantic relationships instead. Brigham Young University conducted a study into this very subject, investigating to what extent technology in interfering and how damaging it can be to romance. The conclusion of that study was not only did technology hurt your relationship, it could affect your psychological health too. Specifically, the term "technoference" was used in this study and it discovered that the higher the technoference, the more conflict and relationship dissatisfaction you're likely to experience.

Why We Need to Step Away from Technology

Relationships, as we know it today, are very different from what they were a decade ago. The introduction of smartphones and social media has rapidly changed the way we connect with the world and the people around us. As our mobile devices offer greater features, our addiction to them seems to grow in equal measure. All you have to do is observe on your next train or bus commute home just how many people are glued to their devices throughout the journey.

The statistics revealed by Pew Research Centre showed

that a whopping 67% of people often checked their devices even if it didn't ring, while 44% of people slept with their phones next to them. And then, there's 29% of those surveyed who said they simply "couldn't live" without their mobile devices. It is safe to say that most relationships in the 21st century have a constant "third party" in them in the form of digital devices.

While mobile phones have done our lives a world of good and made connecting with people no matter where they are in the world, when it comes to *real life connections,* we need to step away from our digital devices in order to connect with the person who is right next to us instead of on a screen. It is important to digitally disconnect when spending quality time with your partner because when you're distracted by what's happening on your phone, you're missing out on crucial moments, important information and body language signals which your partner may be trying to convey about what they're feeling.

When you disconnect from what's digital, you're able to connect to the physical. Being present and engaged in your relationship and your surroundings is what your relationship needs, not another social media tweet, Instagram post or Facebook update. A healthy relationship needs communication that is happening in real life, not over text messages. In fact, more fights tend to happen over text message miscommunication than if you were to have an actual conversation, because of how quickly and easily messages can be misread or misinterpreted. Don't use text messages to apologize over disagreements, or to argue with your partner. Do it in person because that essential human connection is what is needed to strengthen your relationship. The more dependent you are on technology, the more disconnected from your partner you will feel over time.

Technology has also made it possible for many of us to work remotely, even when we're away from the office. Responding to emails, following up with clients, organizing meetings, it has now become possible for us to bring work with us everywhere we go. Sometimes, this can prove to be a convenience, but other times it just makes it that much more difficult for us to achieve work-life balance, especially when it takes time away from your partner because you can't be present with them when your mind is focused on work instead. It makes you wonder whether being connected digitally all the time is really such a good thing for any of us.

How to Disconnect Digitally and Start Being Engaged Physically in Your Relationship

You don't need a big romantic gesture or a fancy, overpriced dinner to show your partner that you love them. You could show just how much they mean to you without ever spending a cent, all you need to do is simply spend more time with them. Give them your full attention and for those few moments that you spend together, make a commitment to be there and be present. Everything else can wait for a moment.

Here's how you can start digitally disconnecting from your devices to improve your communication as a couple:

- **Set Expectations -** Understandably, disconnecting for an entire day or maybe two is not entirely possible for many couples. The key is to find a middle ground that works for both of you by setting expectations. Start by committing to setting aside one hour each day to spend time with each other without your phones, tablets or computers present. Both partners need to come to an agreement to commit to spending this quality time together, and as it becomes a habit, you can slowly move onto increasing the amount of time spent, provided you're both in agreement with it.

- **Set Tech-Free Zones -** Set up some zones around the home which are "tech-free". The bedroom for example, or the family room, maybe even the dining room during meal times could be set up as spaces where you're not going to use technology during the times that you're there. This allows you to focus instead of having conversations with your partner instead of constantly checking for the next email or social media update. This could be great for improving your sleep patterns too.

- **Turn It Off -** Putting your phone aside or putting it on silent alone is not going to be enough. That's not digitally disconnecting, because as soon as you hear it vibrating, your attention is going to be immediately drawn towards your phone, wondering what alert or update you just received. No, you need to *turn it off* completely. No ifs, no buts. Off.

- **Do Activities Together Which Don't Involve Your Phones** – A great way to get your mind off your phone is to have it focused on something else. At least a few times in a week, do an activity with your partner and throughout the duration of that activity, make it a commitment that neither of you is going to check your mobile phones until it's over.

You don't have to completely cut yourself off from the digital world. The key to a happy, healthy relationship is to find that balance so that your relationships don't get neglected along the way. After all, couples from a decade ago managed to survive without these fancy digital devices that we have today. You can do the same.

Chapter 9: Skill #9 – Apologizing Mindfully

When you apologize to your partner, how often do you *mean* it? Apologizing and saying all the right words is easy, but apologizing *mindfully* requires that you think about what you're saying and say it with emotion and feeling. Mindful apologies are more meaningful because of the sincerity and genuine feeling that is involved. Anyone can just utter the words *I'm sorry* for the sake of doing so, or because it is expected of them. But is an apology for the sake of doing so *really* an apology at all?

The Purpose of an Apology

An apology is supposed to serve two purposes. The first is to show remorse over your actions, and the second is to acknowledge that your actions may have caused someone else a lot of hurt and pain.

For a healthy relationship to exist, you must learn how to apologize mindfully. Nobody is perfect, and along the way, we are bound to commit mistakes. Yes, mistakes do get made along the way, but the difference lies in the way that you handle what happens after those mistakes have been made, how you restore the harmony and the trust in your relationship, and how you let your partner know that you are genuinely sorry for what happened.

An apology symbolizes your willingness to admit your mistake, and that alone is a step in the right direction. There are many people who simply refuse to admit when they are wrong because they let their pride and ego get in the way. They would rather let their relationship suffer than to have to admit they are wrong. You don't want to be one of these people. When you are willing to admit that you've made a mistake and own up to it, you're giving your partner (or anyone else for that matter) the opportunity to communicate with you so you can start working through your feelings together, to discuss what is acceptable behavior and what isn't moving forward.

Apologies let your partner know that you realize what you did was wrong, and that your behavior may have been unacceptable. An apology lets your partner know that you are ready to work on building and re-establishing that bond in your relationship. It allows the healing process to begin and reassures your partner that you do care about their feelings and you're willing to work on improving your flaws.

What Happens If You Don't Apologize?

Needless to say, one of the biggest consequences of refusing to apologize when you've made a mistake is the deterioration of your relationship. Your partner may be patient and forgiving, but the biggest mistake you could commit is to take that for granted. Everyone has their limits, even the most patient person. One day, when your partner has had enough, they will eventually pack up and leave. You don't want to wait until it gets to that point.

Not apologizing is going to cause a lot of hurt and animosity, tension, stress, and worst of all, emotional pain. Anger can do more damage to a person's soul than you realize, and the words you say cannot be taken back once it has been put out there.

Why Some People Find Apologies So Hard?

We know that apologies are necessary to repair and restore relationships. Yet, so many people struggle to utter these two simple words and to mean what they say. Aside from ego and pride which gets in the way, why are apologies sometimes so difficult?

For one thing, it takes a lot of effort and courage to admit that you were in the wrong. In doing that, you take on the blame and put yourself in a position that is vulnerable, which a lot of people actively want to avoid. Another reason why apologies are so difficult for some people is because they may be ashamed or embarrassed about the way that they behaved. They know what they did or said was wrong, and they are so ashamed of their actions that they can't bring themselves to face it.

And then there's arrogance, which falls right along the same lines as ego and pride does. The only way to overcome this is to let go of your need to always be right and to feel superior. After all, when dealing with someone that you love, do you really feel the need to be better than they are?

How to Start Apologizing Mindfully

Saying *I'm sorry* alone simply isn't enough. An apology is not going to mean anything if you don't put any emotion into it. If you're only going to apologize because it's what you're "supposed to do", then you're better off not apologizing at all.

Apologizing mindfully can open the door to much better communication and healing in the relationship, and here's is how you do it:

- **Don't Just Feel Remorse, Express It** - Put emotion and feeling behind your words when you apologize. With the emotional intelligence skills, you have developed, empathize and put yourself in your partner's shoes. How would you feel if you were in their situation? Being authentic and genuine with your apology requires you to feel the hurt that they could be feeling, and in doing so, feel remorse over having hurt them in that way.

- **Don't Wait to Apologize** - It is also equally important to apologize as soon as you realize that you were in the wrong. Don't wait until tomorrow, next week or next month to do it, because it then loses all meaning. The hurt and the damage has been done, and if you don't do something at that moment to fix it, it might end up being a case of too little too late.

- **Accepting Responsibility** - Empathy is once more going to come into play here as you accept responsibility for what you did wrong. When you realize just how much hurt you've caused your partner or how you've wronged them, let them know that you understand how your actions have made them feel. For example, expressing *I'm sorry, I know I hurt you when I snapped at you in anger. I was wrong, I shouldn't have done that and I am truly sorry.*

- **Forgo the Excuses -** A mindful apology is a sincere apology which comes from the heart. Which means you need to forgo the excuses and attempts at trying to justify your behavior. There are no excuses for hurting the person that you love, and if that happens, you need to accept responsibility for your actions and don't try to shift the blame or make excuses which could only weaken your apology and make it seem less sincere.

Chapter 10: Skill #10 – No Judgment Zone

Judgment. It is among the most damaging forces that a relationship could experience, aside from anger. Whenever you judge someone, especially your partner, the message that you're sending them is that you don't accept them for who they are. In turn, the hurt emotions that they experience from your judgment will build up resentment within them and over time, the relationship will fall apart.

Dr. Margaret Paul (Ph.D.), a relationship expert, pointed out that judgment, this subconscious behavior we engage in without even realizing that we're doing it, is something that "erodes intimacy" in a couple's relationship. Regardless if it is whether you judge others, or even if you were judging yourself, Paul points out that judgment causes a lot of problems in a relationship.

Why Judgment Is Such A Damaging Quality

Each time that you judge your partner, you make them feel embarrassed, insecure, perhaps even anxious and tense. When they experience this form of rejection from you, as a way to protect themselves, they will close themselves off to you because they don't feel secure enough to open up freely and be themselves. This is how judgment erodes intimacy.

In a loving relationship, you should not have to hide who you are. When you judge, you're preventing the other person from truly being themselves. Expecting your partner to live up to your expectations - especially if you have high standards - is unrealistic, and a little bit unfair at the same time. Everyone is different, and no two people are going to be the same. Yes, you and your partner may have several things in common which drew you together in the first place, but you are *still* two different people. Expecting them to live up to your expectations and then judging them when they fail to, is unfair.

Mother Teresa once said that if you spend far too much time judging people, then you have no time left to love them. When a relationship is new and exciting, it is easy to fall in love when everything seems to be going perfectly. Everyone always puts their best foot forward and presents their best qualities because they're trying to impress their partner. As the relationship continues to progress, that's when all the other behaviors, traits, and quirky personality elements start to show through. Some you may find endearing, others you may find annoying and it is during this phase that judgmental thoughts start to swim around in your head.

Why Do We Judge the People We Love?

You may not be doing it on purpose. Sometimes you may not even realize you're doing it all. The human brain is wired to judge those who we perceive to be different from ourselves, and when your partner behaves differently in a way that you would, judgment surfaces.

Judgment could be in the form of comparing your partner to other men, your friend's partners, thinking that you know better than them and trying to change them to be more like what you expect them to be. Each time you find yourself judging your partner, take note of the way you feel at that moment. You're likely to feel less connected or close to them as you normally would. Why? Because judgment is creating a separation barrier between the two of you. What's worse is that your partner often may not even realize they are under scrutiny as you silently judge them, and they won't understand why there has been a shift in your emotions or the way that you feel.

How to Stop Judging the People We Love

Now that we know that judgment is a damaging force in any relationship (not just the romantic ones), the next question that we need to ask ourselves is *how do we stop*? You can still save your relationship before it's too late, here's what you need to do to stop judging your partner:

- **Don't Expect Them to Be Like You** - Your partner is doing their best, and giving it their best in your relationship. They're doing the best that they know how, based on their experiences and what they've been through in life so far. Nobody would purposely be on their worst behavior. This is what you need to remind yourself of, and why each time you find yourself about to judge your partner, remember that *they are not like you*. The sooner you let go of that expectation, the quicker you'll be able to learn how to stop judging the one that you say you love.

- **Listen to What They're Saying -** When we often find ourselves judging our partners, we're not listening. You've already mentally blocked yourself off and all you care about at that moment is how *you feel* and what *you think.* This especially happens during an argument, when you disagree with what your partner is saying and you judge them for it. Again, you're going to have to rely on emotional intelligence to get you through this. Empathize, take a step back and try to *actively listen* to what they are telling you and see the truth in what they say. Understand that whatever it is they are telling you, it is how they perceive things from their point of view, and there's nothing wrong with that. Keep an open mind and you will learn how to judge less.

- **You're Not There to Manage Their Life -** Everyone is entitled to live their life the way that they want. A relationship is two people coming together and sharing their lives together, both ups, downs, good and bad. That's the beauty of a relationship, that two people who are so different can come together and blend their lives together. To judge your partner less, sometimes you need to focus less on trying to manage their lives. You're there to love them and support them, not correct their lives and try to micromanage everything to a point that you judge them when they fail to live up to your expectations.

- **Let Go of Expectations -** And of course, you need to let go of your expectations. Nothing is going to be a bigger let down than for you to set high standards that are almost impossible to meet, especially for your partner. They are not obligated to live life according to your rules, and you need to let go of expecting far too much from them. Expect them to be nothing but themselves, and you'll have a much happier relationship at the end of the day.

- **Focus Less On Their Flaws, And More On Their Good Qualities -** Another downfall of the human brain is that we're, again, programmed to focus more on the negative. Which is why it always seems much easier to be negative and see everything that is wrong instead of focusing on the positive.

Remaining positive is hard work and requires constant effort. To learn to judge your partner less, start focusing on their good traits instead. Remind yourself of all the reasons you fell in love in the first place. Make this a consistent and conscious effort and over time, you will increase your compassion rather than your judgment.

Chapter 11: Skill #11 – Working on Yourself First

This is going to be a very important chapter as you work on your self-improvement. If you want to become an improved version of yourself and improve your romantic relationships, then you don't just need to focus on improving the external aspects, you need to focus on what's within, too. The very reason you picked up this book is that you want to improve the communication that happens between you and your partner to become the better version of yourself for the sake and health of your relationship.

Where to Begin When It Comes to Self-Improvement

It starts with reshaping your mindset. Changing your mindset is an important step if you want to see visible change taking place in your relationship. Lao Tzu once uttered the wise words, *"If you correct your mind, the rest of your life will eventually fall into place."* That sentence alone highlights just how vital it is to reshape your mind; how powerful this one tactic can be.

Developing a positive mindset is something that you need to make a part of your life. A happy, healthy relationship is not just going to fall into your lap, you are going to have to work hard to get there. A shift is all it takes to start seeing things in a brand-new light, which is when meaningful change starts to happen. It is important to begin cultivating a better mindset if you want to improve yourself because:

- **It Will Help to Improve Your Focus -** One of the things you're going to need to work on improving is to minimize the negativity that is going on inside your mind. Yes, we all have it, we're all guilty of the noisy, negative chatter that often holds us back and prevents us from seeing the good in others (or ourselves). When your mind is not as clouded by negativity, you will be able to focus on seeing the good things that are happening in your life and learn to appreciate them more.

- **It Improves Your Self-Esteem** - A healthy self-esteem is what you're after, because in the long-run, it will lead to much higher levels of satisfaction in your everyday life and in your relationship.

Self-Improvement Begins with You

The choice to improve yourself starts right now, at this very moment. You have the choice to improve your life today and here is how you begin reshaping your mindset for the better:

- **Learning to Be More Flexible** - Learning to be flexible is an important step towards building a healthier, more positive way of thinking because if you don't, you will find it difficult and frustrating to overcome bumps in the road when things may not be going your way. You can't control everything, especially when it comes to relationships, and learning to be flexible is how you cope with the ups and downs and challenges that come your way. Being flexible is how you learn to work better together with your partner as a team, the way that it should be.

- **Stop Focusing On Your Failures** - The mistakes of the past have a way of haunting us if we don't find a way to deal with them and let them go. This baggage that we carry with us and bring into the new relationships that we forge are not healthy for either party. Reshaping your mind includes changing the way you see failures because as you work towards improving yourself, you are going to have to overcome a few challenges which may sometimes take a few setbacks and tries before you get it right. Instead of viewing failures as "failures", see them as learning lessons instead and use them as a gauge of what works and what doesn't.

- **Find Something That Inspires You Daily** - Begin cultivating a positive mindset for your self-improvement by focusing on something each day that inspires you. Wake up each morning and make the first thing that you see something that is going to inspire you for the rest of the day, like a positive quote or image for example. It could be something as simple as a quote or saying that stirs up emotions within you, or maybe even images of inspirational individuals you would love to emulate. Put them around your home or at your work station in the office, places where it would be hard to miss so you can constantly be reminded of it.

- **Positive Talk, Positive Thoughts -** Your thoughts have the power to influence you in more ways than you know. To start cultivating and reshaping your mindset towards self-improvement, you need to start pushing out every negative thought about yourself out of your mind and replace with positive thoughts instead. You're not doing your relationship any good if all you can bring to it is negativity, because it will affect both you and your partner in a bad way. If you're finding it difficult to list down the positive qualities about yourself, turn to your partner for help and get them to list what they think are your most positive attributes. Toss out negativity one day at a time. Always look at the silver lining, train yourself to do it. It can be hard to see how they could help, but positive affirmations do remarkable feats when it comes to shifting a person's perception and mindset. The most successful, prominent individuals - motivational speakers for example - in this world are constantly talking about how positive affirmations can do wonders to change your life. If it works for them, it can work for you too.

- **Remember to Love Yourself -** This is perhaps the most important practical self- improvement tip you can take away with you from this chapter. If you don't love yourself, how do you expect others to love you? Your partner is in a relationship with you right now *because they love you.* If you are going to constantly rely on others to feel worthy, you will never become the improved version of yourself that you long to be. If you can easily list all the things you don't like about yourself at the snap of your finger, you can do the same when it comes to listing the qualities you do love about yourself.

Chapter 12: Skill #12 – Using Irony to Diffuse Unpleasant Situations

Forging connections to today's modern world isn't as simple as one might expect. We are surrounded by all sorts of technological devices and gadgets which are supposed to bring us closer to the ones we love and the people who matter, yet somehow we seem to be more *disconnected* than ever, and we struggle to form intimate human connections sometimes. Talk about irony, right?

Irony. It works well in some contexts. But is using irony to diffuse an unpleasant situation in a relationship a good thing?

Types of Irony

In general, there are three different categories of irony, which are dramatic, verbal, and situational. Verbal irony is what happens when a person's intention is the exact *opposite* of what they are saying. For example, if you were caught in the middle of a traffic jam, you might say something like "I love how smooth the traffic is!".

Situational irony, on the other hand, is when the outcome of a situation is completely *different* from what you expected it to be. Situational irony is something which is used in a lot of sitcoms. One example of situational irony at play is when you plan an elaborate surprise birthday party for your friend, only to realize that her birthday is *next* month and not on the day that you threw her party on.

And then there is dramatic irony, in which also we see a lot of in movies. This is when you, as the audience, already know something that the character or person in the movie does not. In a horror movie, for example, you know it is a bad idea to go into a dark and deserted room, yet the person in the movie walks into the room anyway only to realize what do you know? Turns out it *was* a bad idea.

In a sitcom or movie situation, irony can bring a few laughs, and even make an unpleasant situation seem funny. Irony is even used in literature quite a bit too, and depending on the context which the author uses it, sometimes it can produce a few laughs in the reader.

In a real-life romantic situation, is irony necessarily the best approach to take? The thing about irony is that it can serve as a defense mechanism for some people's ego. It is used along the similar lines of sarcasm, where we use verbal irony to protect ourselves in a way from getting hurt or embarrassed. These people would rather have others laugh *with* them than *at* them. But if you're going to resort to using irony all the time in a relationship to help diffuse unpleasant situations, your partner might not necessarily see that as a good thing. You could be perceived as not taking the situation seriously enough if you're going to always go around making jokes about it, especially if your partner is trying to have a serious discussion with you.

There are also some people, who resort to irony because they want to avoid conflict. Conflicts tend to make some people uncomfortable, and rather than face the problem head-on, they use irony to try and diffuse the situation instead. Again, using this approach might not always be a good thing in a romantic relationship. If your partner is the serious type who would rather talk things out and resolve the matter then and there, and your approach is to use irony to deal with the situation, that could only end up causing more problems. Your partner may get frustrated at your lack of perceived willingness to resolve the situation, and you will get frustrated too because you're actively trying to avoid conflict and dealing with it in the way that you think is best.

Should We Use Irony in Our Relationships?

Relationships are a complicated system. If your partner has a sense of humor, yes it can certainly be used to help diffuse unpleasant situations, because it helps the two of you to see the funny side of things. Perhaps even get a couple of good laughs or two. But as for whether irony is the *best* approach to take? Well, perhaps not all the time. It can be either a good thing or a bad thing, depending on how you perceive it and how you use it within your relationship.

The thing about relationships is that it involves two people coming together, trying to work together to create harmony. When there's a disagreement over the way things are done, middle ground and compromise must be created so that both parties end up happy and satisfied with the outcome. When you know that in certain situations, using irony might upset your partner even more, so try to meet them halfway and figure out another approach to resolving the unpleasant situation.

Instead of irony, what might be better is to use humor to help relieve the tension that is sometimes felt from time to time. Being able to laugh what brings people closer together, and having a sense of humor has always been recognized as an important quality to have in a long-term relationship. Humor is merely about the funny things that get said, it is also about the things that you do together as a couple. It is about having *fun* in each other's presence, and indulging in activities that make you laugh.

A sense of humor helps you see the happier, lighter side of life and revel in it, and that is what makes it a much better approach to take than irony. We will talk more about humor in the next chapter and what it can do for your relationship.

Chapter 13: Skill 13 – A Couple That Laughs Together, Stays Together

If you could choose what the absolute favorite was, what would it be? Would it be that you laugh together a lot as a couple? Have you experienced that laughter which leaves you in stitches? Cracking up so hard that you can't help the tears from pouring down your cheeks and your sides aching so hard you feel as if you could never stand up again? That kind of laughter is a magical thing that can bring two people together in exceptional ways.

Picture what it would be like for a moment, to be in a relationship that had no laughter. No sense of humor, no shared memories that leave you both smiling and laughing at the very recollection. How would that make you feel?

Laughter has the power to heal and it can touch a deep emotion within us that no other emotion can. Research conducted by the University of North Carolina revealed that couples who shared laughs together had a much happier relationship because of the closeness that they felt and the support they received from their partner.

A lot of times, the challenges that we go through in life boils down to our capacity to handle it, the way we perceive it and the relationships that we have in our lives that help us get through it. The stronger the bond you share with your partner, the better your ability to communicate and work through issues as a couple.

How Laughter Can Benefit Your Romantic Relationship

A couple who laughs together share a much stronger bond, and because of that bond, they are able to overcome challenges and conflicts that crop up in their relationship much better than couples who don't have a bond that is that strong. Many couples have listed a sense of humor as one of the qualities that they look for in a long-term partner, because if you can't have fun with the person that you love, could you imagine yourself in a long-term relationship with them?

The old saying *laughter is the best medicine* actually holds a lot of truth to it. Being able to laugh heartily is a sign of happiness, and if laughter is something that you share a lot of in your relationship, that's a sign that your relationship is a happy one. Among the benefits that you stand to derive from having a sense of humor in your relationship include:

- **It Makes You Feel Physically Much Better -** Have you ever noticed how good you feel after a good laugh? How your spirits have just lifted and suddenly things don't seem so bad? Laughter is one of the most healing experiences we can go through as a human being, and it can physically do wonders for you better than any modern day medicine can. It releases endorphins in your body, which is the body's natural feel-good chemical, lowers your blood pressure, puts you in a relaxed state and even helps to lower stress.

- **It Lowers Your Inhibitions -** It's hard to feel defensive, angry or on the edge when you're feeling good and laughing. Especially if you're doing it with your partner, which is why humor is a much better situation diffuser than irony ever will be.

- **It Helps to Improve Your Communication -** Want to improve your communication between you and your partner? Use humor and laughter to do it. When a situation is tense and you think it's not going well, sometimes, a well-timed appropriate joke can help to break the tension and bring a smile to your partner's face. When you learn to laugh together about some of the challenges that go on in your life, it can sometimes help to put things into perspective, and even provide you with a creative solution you might not otherwise have thought of in your otherwise tense situation.

- **It Can Bring Back the Excitement In Your Relationship -** Things can often feel boring and stagnant after a while in a long term relationship. Especially if you or your partner are the kinds of people who often need excitement once in a while to keep things interesting. Having to deal with problems and challenges that go along with being in a relationship can sometimes take its toll. Well, guess what, laughter can help with that too. Not only does sharing these moments that make you laugh help to bring you closer together as a couple, but it can also even remind you of why you were attracted to your partner in the first place, and perhaps even make you fall in love with them all over again.

- **It Adds Another Layer of Intimacy -** Sharing inside jokes that no one else but you and your partner understand adds another layer of intimacy to your relationship. It's that knowledge of the special connection that you share, almost like a secret world that only the two of you know about, and when you look at each other, a smile, nod or wink can instantly create a surge of affection.

- **Helps to Restore Positivity in Your Relationship** - Not only does laughter help to diffuse difficult situations in your relationship, but it can also help to diffuse negative emotions too. It is impossible to feel that cloud of negativity when you're sharing a good laugh together.

- **Good Times Become Even Better** - Good times are made even better when there's laughter in the mix. Think about the moments when you and your partner were having a good time, and when you shared several laughs together, how much better those moments felt. You could look back for years to come and those memories would still bring a smile to your face. It gives you good stories to reminisce about too, when you say, "*Hey, remember that time when we…*" and laughing together all over again is only going to strengthen your bond even more.

Chapter 14: Skill #14 – Don't Neglect the Sexual Aspect

The sexual aspect of a relationship can cause a lot of worry and anxiety for many. Thanks to social media and movies and the unrealistic expectations they have set for romantic relationships, the pressure to perform in the bedroom can be overwhelming. Without proper communication going on, a relationship can quickly break down in the bedroom thanks to stress, anxiety, worry, and the fear that you're not living up to your partner's expectations.

Anxiety Over Sexual Relationships

Couples who are dealing with sexual intimacy issues are often susceptible to experiencing anxiety and fear, along with a wide range of worries that accompany those emotions. Among the things that may be running through a person's head when they worry about their intimate relationships include:

- They worry about being judged by their partner

- They suffer from low self-esteem and constantly find themselves worried about everything

- They constantly need to be reassured, sometimes on a daily basis and no matter how much your partner does his or her best to reassure you, it never feels like it is enough.

- They are unable to enjoy the sexual aspect of their relationship because they are more worried about whether they doing it right and whether they're satisfying you enough.

- They find it difficult to believe that their partner is

happy with the sexual aspect of the relationship, despite the reassurance.

- They may find it difficult to be intimate because they are so full of worry.

- They experience a decrease in their sex drive as a direct result of that stress and worry.

Are you or your partner experiencing any of the symptoms or signs above? Then what you could be dealing with is sexual relationship anxiety. If left unchecked, this anxiety will only lead to mistrust and the inability to connect with your partner in the bedroom the way that you should as a couple. Sexual relationship anxiety can put a lot of pressure and stress on both people in the relationship, not just the one who is living with it, but also the one that has to deal with the one who has it. Excessive worry can lead to destructive relationship behaviors and over a prolonged period, it can cause the relationship to break down because one or both parties feel like they are not able to deal with the stress of it all anymore.

How to Recognize the Signs That Your Partner Is Suffering from Sexual Relationship Anxiety

Anxiety is an emotional state of being, and this means that different individuals will experience anxiety in different ways. If you suspect that you or your partner could be dealing with this, some common tell-tale signs to look out for include difficulty expressing their emotions. Common words that could possibly be expressed by your partner if he or she is going through anxiety would be worry, fear, dread, apprehension, distress, overwhelmed, pressure, stress, being on edge, and more. If they regularly express these emotions which are followed by signs of physical distress, that will signal to you that something is not right, because thought patterns like these are very commonly expressed by those who are dealing with anxiety.

If your partner is constantly expressing that they are feeling overwhelmed, that is something you need to take seriously because it is a symptom of anxiety. They feel overwhelmed because again, it is linked back to how they obsessed and overthink almost everything. You would be surprised that they can obsess even about the smallest, possible detail which may seem insignificant to you. Things like they feel that they're not good kissers, or that their body is not as perfect as they want it to be, or even that they feel they are not good in bed for example. As a result of overthinking, they get worked up and feel that they are unable to cope because they are not able to think straight and think rationally in the situation.

Anxiety over sexual relationships is a very real problem that is not to be taken lightly. Anxiety, in general, is an actual mental health issue that should never be dismissed with statements such as "it's all in your head." Anxiety is a serious issue that requires serious help.

What You Can Do to Help Your Partner Through It

Improving communication overall includes being able to communicate about the sexual aspect of your relationship. You may find that talking about all the other issues that take place is much easier than having to talk about your sex life. Yes, it may be a tough conversation to have, but if you're going to improve your overall communication as a couple, this is something you're going to have to learn to talk about too.

When your partner is dealing with sexual relationship anxiety, they are constantly worried and fearful. These are the two primary emotions that they are feeling. This constant state of worry and fear makes them less aware and unable to tune in to the needs of their partner because they are unable to focus on anything except their own worries and fears. When they are in this state, they find it difficult to trust and connect with anyone, even their partners. They may even feel that you are not being there for them in the way that they need because they are not thinking clearly.

When your partner is going through a moment like this, do your best to approach the situation calmly so you can help them to calm down. Avoid being equally emotional, because that could just escalate the situation when they are already in a highly emotional state of mind. You need to remain calm and steady before attempting to calm your partner down. Encourage them to talk to you about what they are feeling. The best thing for you to do in this situation would be to approach your partner with kindness and empathy (emotional intelligence comes into play here again). Remind them that you are not going anywhere, and if they need someone to talk to, encourage them to trust you enough to open up. It can be difficult to remain positive when things are difficult and challenging, so what you can do to help is to keep reminding yourself that your partner is only acting this way because of their sexual relationship anxiety, and this is not who they really are.

Other things you can do to reassure your partner and improve communication in the bedroom include:

- Creating a safe space to talk about things in a way that allows both of you to be comfortable enough to open up

- Showing your partner respect and support

- Notice what is important to them, what they need and make that a priority.

- Be genuine with your compliments and reassurances, so your partner knows that you're not just saying that because you're trying to get things to go your way in the bedroom.

- Open up to *them* about the way that *you feel.* Share your own worries, fears and needs so that they know they are not the only ones going through this alone.

Chapter 15: Skill #15 – Getting Some Space

It is easy to lose yourself in a romantic relationship. Being caught up in the romance, trying to please your partner and keep them happy and wanting to spend as much time around them as possible can make you forget what life was like *before* you ventured into the relationship. You could easily get caught up in wanting to do all the things that your partner loves to do that you eventually neglect your own interests over time.

Why it becomes easy to lose ourselves in another person is because their happiness can take priority over ours - especially in the beginning. Because we love them, we want to do everything we can to make them happy and that becomes our number one priority. In doing so, we forget that there are other aspects of our lives that bring us meaning and happiness, even before we found our partners.

Why Getting Space Is Important

Especially when you live with your partner, it is important to find some time to do things independently and on your own. Neglecting the things that you like to do - hobbies, interests, passions, and activities - puts you in a dangerously unhealthy relationship. What's going to happen when your partner isn't around? You're going to find yourself completely at a loss, possibly even losing a sense of who you are, which has often happened with a lot of relationships where couples rely too heavily on each other.

The healthiest relationships are the ones where the couples are able to find a balance. They have common shared interests which allow them to bond and grow together as a couple, but they also have other interests which are independent of just themselves. These are the couples who enjoy each other's company, but at the same time are perfectly happy and content to enjoy their own company every now and then. It is important in every relationship that you maintain a sense of independence because:

- **You Need to Maintain Your Individuality -** If you're always so consumed by just the things that your partner loves to do, you're losing a lot of what makes you unique. The special qualities about yourself are part of the reason why your partner fell in love with you in the first place. It is part of your identity and who you are as a person. Maintaining a relationship with yourself is just as important as maintaining a relationship with another person. If you don't get to know yourself, you will never be able to love yourself.

- **You Are Able to Contribute More to Your Relationship -** You may be part of a relationship, but you are also your own person, and the individual qualities that make you great are what you contribute to making your relationship even better. When you're comfortable and happy with who you are as a person, you'll realize that you have so much more to offer. You don't need another individual to make you whole because *you are already whole enough.* Having your significant other in your life is just adding another element which brings you more happiness because now you have someone to share your life with.

- **It Keeps Your Relationship Alive -** If you're only going to be consumed by your partner's likes and interests, pretty soon you'll find that you have quickly run out of things to talk about. Especially in a long-term relationship. It may be more fun to do things with your partner, but when you push yourself out of your comfort zone, you'll gain an amazing new sense of freedom that you forgot was once there. You used to indulge in your activities and hobbies once upon a time before you found your partner, and when you continue doing that, perhaps even picking up new activities and interests along the way, you'll have even more things to share and talk about with your partner.

- **It Helps You Maintain Your Confidence -** When you become far too reliant on someone else to do things, you could lose your sense of confidence along the way. When you suddenly find yourself in a situation where you may have to do certain things alone, it suddenly feels difficult to engage in these activities with confidence. That can happen when you make someone else your focus, and what a lot of couples fail to realize is this can be a cause for the deterioration in their relationship. You feel bound to your partner for the wrong reasons, and sometimes you may even be afraid to leave a bad relationship because you don't want to find yourself alone again. This is why it is important to maintain your own independence, to create some space every now and then from your partner to do your own thing. It reminds you that you are capable of being on your own *and* in a healthy relationship, and you're capable of thriving in both situations.

- **You Need to Work On Your Own Happiness** - You owe it to yourself to work on your own happiness. If you rely on external forces for your happiness - and this includes your partner - you will find it hard to hold onto that happiness, especially when those sources are not around. Happiness needs to come from within and to do that, you need to work on yourself. When you feel genuinely happy, you're less stressed and tense, which then reduces the arguments that might occur. Your happiness should never be put in the hands of someone else, what your partner should be is *added joy*, instead of being the only reason for that happiness. The happiness that comes from within is the one that is going to last forever, and when you can bring that happiness into your relationship and share it with your partner, that's when the relationship grows stronger and flourishes.

While it is natural to want to share everything about your life with your partner, it is important to realize that not *everything* needs to be shared. In fact, having time away from each other and missing each other will only serve to make you appreciate your partner even more when you do reunite again.

Chapter 16: Skill #16 – Setting Goals Together

A goal can set you down a very powerful path. As a couple, creating shared goals to work towards is one of the most powerful exercises you could do to improve not just your connection, but your communication. Working on shared goals together can be fun, especially because there is nothing better than doing things and sharing successful accomplishments with the person that you love.

Goals help to turn that everything you envision as a couple into a reality. Every couple wants to see their relationship going somewhere, and setting goals to work towards will help give you something to focus on.

What Exactly Is a Goal?

A goal is defined as a desire to achieve a result which you have envisioned in your mind. Think about all the things you had planned to do, especially as a couple, but haven't quite gotten around to doing them just yet. Could that be because you didn't have a goal in mind and an action plan to help you get to that desired outcome? A goal helps you stay on track because it reminds you why you got started to begin with.

Goals give you the focus, the knowledge, and the ability to organize both your time and resources so you are making the most out of every waking moment of the day. It gives you perspective in your life and helps you shape the decisions that you make from this point moving forward as a couple. Goal setting with your partner is even more fulfilling and rewarding because you know that you're not doing this alone. Having that support in the form of your partner can help to motivate and fuel your desire to succeed and vice versa.

Why Is It Important to Set Goals as a Couple?

Creating a shared vision and goals for yourselves, and as a couple is important. If you've ever found yourself in past relationships where you and your partner were on completely different pages, you'll know just how stressful it can be and what a strain it can be on a relationship. Or perhaps envision a moment when you've set a goal for what you want to achieve out of a relationship but along the way you struggled and felt frustrated because you felt you weren't receiving the support that you needed from your partner. Not being on the same page with you about your goal probably made it that much harder to communicate, which only increased the sense of frustration which was being felt.

For a relationship to survive and thrive in the long term, goal setting as a couple is something that is absolutely a necessity. Without goals, you may quickly find that your relationship loses a sense of purpose or direction along the way, especially when it reaches a point where it stagnates and doesn't feel like it is moving forward in the way that you hoped. Without that sense of purpose, a relationship can quickly crack under the strain.

How to Start Setting Goals as A Couple

Setting goals as a couple is about creating a vision that you share together and then making a commitment to achieve that vision. Setting goals as a couple is not at all complicated, and in fact, here are some simple but effective strategies to help you get started:

- **Defining the Areas of Importance -** There's a lot of things going on in a relationship, and while you may be tempted to tackle all these areas, try to take it one step at a time. Goal setting should start in the areas which matter the most to both of you as a couple. These areas could be for example marriage, family, finances, kids, or even buying your first home together. It can be anything that you want, as long as it is an area that you think is important to your relationship.

- **Talk About It and Write It Down -** Set some time to sit down and have a discussion about what goals you and your partner hope to get out of the relationship. Write down each goal that you have (ask your partner to do the same), and then compare the goals which you have written down and see if you've got anything in common. If there are different goals that you both would like to achieve, brainstorm what you can do to meet each other halfway, or help each other to realize these goals so both parties are happy and satisfied with the outcome.

- **Keep an Open Mind -** It is only natural that you and your partner are bound to have goals which are different. You're two very different people, with different perspectives and visions about where you see the relationship going. Keep an open mind when comparing goals with your partner and communicate with each other about why you think a particular goal is important. Understanding and listening to each other's point of view show that you are not dismissive towards each other's needs. Some of your partner's goals may not have been something that you would have initially considered, and some of your goals may not have been things that they would have considered.

- **Reflecting On the Goals You've Set -** Once you and your partner have finalized the goals that you would like to begin working on, spend a couple of minutes just reflecting on your goals. Take a good, long look at the goals which you have in front of you and map out the next steps which are needed moving forward to work towards achieving these goals together as a team.

- **Time for Action -** Next, it's time to work together with your partner on devising a plan of action. This is another great opportunity to work on communicating with each other as you begin to talk about how you're going to work through this process together. The action plan that you settle on should be aligned with your goals. If your goal, for example, commits to doing an activity of interest once a month to work on strengthening your bond as a couple, then the action plan should include a list of activities to do, when during the month this should happen and what are the ground rules for this activity. The rules could be no use of mobile phones during that time so you can really enjoy the time you spend with each other. Your action plan does not have to be comprehensive to begin with, it is just to get you started. As you go along, you can add more steps and more actions as ideas start flowing into your mind.

By setting these goals together as a couple, it helps to put the goals in a larger context and gives you a sense of purpose as a couple. The shared victories and successes which you accomplish along the way will give you something to celebrate over, and it also helps to pinpoint which areas of your relationship need working on so you can improve moving forward.

Chapter 17: Skill #17 – Don't' Hold onto Anger

If there is one emotion that is present and exists in everyone, it is anger. It is considered one of our core emotions, like happiness. It happens even to the best people. While anger is a natural emotion, it becomes a problem when it happens more frequently than it should, especially in romantic relationships. It becomes an even *bigger problem* when one or both partners refuse to let go of that anger and move on from it.

Have you ever had moments where you recalled an argument or a confrontation you had, and the mere thought of it just makes your blood boil all over again? That's what anger can do. It makes you hold onto grudges, makes it hard to forgive, let go and move on. Prolonged anger in any relationship, not just the romantic ones, can lead to unhappiness, years of not talking to one another and cause relationships to be ruined over matters which are often not worth it at all. The problem with anger in some people is that they find it hard to let go.

Why Do We Feel Angry?

There could be several reasons why we feel angry. Since each individual is unique, everyone is going to have different triggers which cause anger to spring forth. Some examples of what could be anger triggers in a romantic relationship include the following:

- When you experience unfair treatment

- When you feel you are being treated unkindly

- When you have been lied to

- When promises are broken

- When you feel you are being disrespected

- When you feel powerless or helpless to put a stop to something

- When your partner doesn't seem to "listen" or do the things you expect them to

- When you're disappointed

- When you feel neglected

- When you can't come to an agreement during an argument

- During an argument

- When things are not going your way

There could be so many possible scenarios and situations that could cause a person to get angry or upset about it. Being able to identify your triggers is how you learn to recognize the factors in your relationship that often cause you to get angry. Once you realize what causes you to get angry, the next step is to understand just how big of a problem it is.

When Does Anger Become a Problem in A Relationship?

While anger is not uncommon and is bound to happen in every relationship, there are several indicators to look out for which signal when your anger may start to go from healthy to problematic. Some of these indicators include:

- You find it hard to let go of anger, even over the

smallest of issues, and you let this anger simmer and boil within you until you explode once again and lash out at your partner.

- You find yourself feeling frustrated and sometimes depressed because of repressed anger issues which you may not even be aware of.

- You find it hard to have a happy, meaningful relationship because you constantly find yourself annoyed, frustrated, disgruntled and perhaps even snappy at even the smallest things.

- You hold onto grudges for a very long time because of that anger and you could end up going for days or weeks without speaking to your partner because of it.

- You find it hard to express your anger in healthy ways, preferring to let it bottle up inside you instead which leads to other emotional problems.

- Other people have told you that you have an anger problem, especially your partner.

- You always are pessimistic and negative because of your anger issues.

Often those who have an anger issue do not realize just how problematic it can be. Especially on the people who are closest to them. They don't understand the full extent of just how hurtful angry words and behavior patterns can be, especially for your partner who is around you the most. Dealing with someone who gets angry far too easily is an exhausting ordeal, constantly having to pacify them and soothe them takes up a lot of time and energy. Your partner will eventually grow weary of having to walk on eggshells around you because they don't want to do anything to set you off, and that, over time, will cause the relationship to break down and make communication difficult.

How to Start Learning to Let Go

It is important to realize that all that stuff you get angry about, the things that you're holding a grudge over, it is not worth it. What is *worth it,* however, is your partner. The person you love. The person who is there for you. That is what matters, not your anger. And it certainly isn't worth it to lose someone you love over anger.

The best thing that you could do for your relationship is to learn to let go. Don't expect your partner to "accept" your anger because this is who you are and this is part of your personality. That is entirely the wrong approach to use, and the only thing you are doing is making excuses to justify your behavior without having to do anything to change it. For the sake of your relationship, you are going to have to put in the effort to make a difference if you want to *see* a difference.

- **You Don't Need to Always Be Right -** There's no need for you to always be right and for one very simple reason. It's not worth it. By continuing to indulge in this behavior, you're not helping yourself or your anger issues. You are, in fact, making things much worse. Let go of the desire and the need to always be right. It will get easier over time too, and you'll feel a sense of satisfaction because deep down, you know that it is the right thing to do.

- **No More Room for Excuses -** The more excuses you make, the harder it will be for you to let go of your anger. There will always be a reason for you to *not* let it go. A reason to be angry, a reason to feel annoyed. There will always be a reason as long as you want it to be. Let go of the excuses and you will learn to let go of your anger eventually.

- **Do Activities Which Make You Happy -** The oldest and one of the most effective. People who struggle with anger issues have a lot of misery and unhappiness inside them. The antidote to that unhappiness is - you guessed it - happiness. Indulge in a passion or a hobby, throw yourself into an activity that you love. With a happier state of mind, it makes it easier to think with a clearer head, you don't get as worked up so easily anymore and it becomes much easier to learn how to control your anger issues.

- **Keep A Mood Journal -** One of the problems when it comes to anger is that you're so overwhelmed with all sorts of emotion that it all comes out all at once, especially when you have been keeping it bottled up for so long. Keeping a journal provides you with a safe and private place where you can express every feeling and emotion you have without the fear of being ridiculed or judged. More importantly, it is possible the safest outlet for you to release your feelings of anger with repercussions, without hurting anyone or yourself in the process, especially your partner.

- **Learning to Forgive -** Getting angry is easy. But forgiveness? Well, that's a different story. It takes great inner strength to forgive and be the bigger person, and it is going to take a lot of work, but it will well be worth it. It is a choice that you alone must make. It helps to remind yourself that this is

someone you love and that alone should be enough
of a reason for forgiveness.

Chapter 18: Skill #18 – Sincerity Matters

Communication is a process which takes a lot of work. *A lot of work.* If you're ever in any doubt about that, just remember the last time you and your partner had a conversation that you walked away from feeling extremely let down, heartbroken at being misunderstood, perhaps even feeling angry. How many times during those moments have you found yourself wishing that you could have communicated better with your partner and perhaps the outcome could have been completely different?

If there is one element which could change the way an entire conversation goes, it is sincerity. Couples often struggle to communicate with each other, especially during difficult conversations about challenging issues because sometimes sincerity is lacking. You may not be able to always control the way your partner communicates, but you *can control how you communicate*, and it starts with understanding why sincerity is such an important and necessary element of the communication process.

As human beings who are involved in a romantic relationship, we need two basic necessities to be happy. We need security, and we need to be able to trust the people that we are with. These two elements rely on our partner to play their part, and likewise, we need to do the same for them, and the way to do that is to be sincere in our relationships. Marianne Dainton, a relationship expert at the La Salle University in Philadelphia, explains that while sometimes little white lies are necessary to help maintain a balance in a relationship or to protect our loved ones, not everyone is in agreement with Dainton's theory. That's because, in reality, there is no one who is in a relationship that will ever say they are okay being lied to. *No one.* Lies have been the downfall of many relationships.

Relationship Happiness Boils Down to Sincerity

There are many factors which contribute to the success of a relationship. Empathy, respect, compatibility, communication, honesty, love (of course) and the most underrated quality of all - *sincerity.* A lot of relationships fall apart not because they have fallen out of love with their partner (although sometimes that may be the case), but because the couples felt a lack of sincerity in the relationship.

When a lack of sincerity exists in a relationship, it creates a distance between you and your partner. People can sense when someone isn't being sincere, no matter how well they think they are hiding that fact, but remember that your body language will eventually always give you away. It causes communication problems when two people aren't able to freely express how they feel about each other, and try to cover it up instead with lies and untruths. Hiding things from the people that you love will never bring any benefit, even though you may believe it is for their own good. Once trust has been severed between two people, it is very hard to repair the damage and earn their trust back again.

How to Start Building a Relationship Based on Sincerity

The foundation of a happy relationship cannot be built if one, or both people in that relationship don't fully understand just how valuable sincerity is. What it means to be sincere is that you are always making a choice to act with honesty and truthfulness at all times. That's all it takes. Be honest with yourself, being truthful to who you are, what motivates you, what you value and always choosing to be truthful about it with your partner. This is what sincerity in a relationship means.

If you think that a lack of sincerity could be a problem that your relationship is dealing with right now that's potentially hindering communication between you and your partner, it's time to do something about it. The situation can still be fixed when acted on quickly enough, and here's how you start building a relationship based on sincerity:

- **It's the Promises You Keep That Make a Difference -** Each time you're about to make a promise to your partner, think of this old saying: *Don't make promises that you can't keep.* Making promises to your partner feels good, to see the smile on their face, but each time you make a promise that you can't keep, the disappointment leaves a little scar within them that chips away at their trust in you. Broken promises hurt, a lot and each promise that gets broken will make it harder for your partner to trust you the next time you make another promise, even when you're sincere about it.

- **Back Your Words Up with Actions -** Words alone are not enough to convince your partner of your sincerity if there's no action to back it up. Another apt saying which sums it all up nicely is *actions speak louder than words*. If all you're doing is using words to make your partner feel better but nothing ever gets done, it's the same as making empty promises that you can't keep.

- **Don't Change Who You Are to Fit In -** You won't be able to put on an act forever. You and your partner are very different people, with different circumstances and different values. If you change who you are because you "think" it's what your partner is hoping for or wanting to see from you, that's not a good basis for building a sincere relationship. Your personality is what makes you who you are, and your partner is with you because they love you for *who you are.* You don't have to change just to feel like you fit in, so be sincere to yourself first before you can begin extending that same sincerity to your partner.

- **Don't Say Or Do Anything You Don't Feel Happy About -** If you're not entirely comfortable doing or saying something, then don't say it. Even if it may be what your partner wants to hear from you. Sincerity doesn't exist if you're pretending for the sake of making someone else happy. They may be happy, but you won't be, not in the long run especially. If you do something for your partner, it should be because you *want to*, not because you feel like you're being forced into it. If you're not entirely comfortable doing or saying something, then let your partner know right from the very beginning. They'll understand.

- **Expressing Gratitude Genuinely -** You know that you feel grateful for your partner and appreciate everything that they do. How do you let them know though? Do you just say how grateful you are for them? Or do you show them how grateful you are through your actions? Don't wait for them to have to ask for something, just do it. Help them out around the house, make a busy day less stressful, buy them flowers for no reason. That way, when you tell them how grateful you are to have them in your life, there is sincerity in it because it was backed up by actions.

Chapter 19: Skill #19 – Productive Conflict Helps

Nobody likes arguing with their partner. If we all could avoid arguments at all, we would. Some couples argue more than others do, and while arguments generally have a negative element associated to it, but there is such a thing as productive conflict, where arguing may actually be a good thing for your relationship.

In fact, in a study conducted by Joseph Grenny and David Maxfield conducted an online study entitled *Able Arguers* in 2012 which discovered that the happiest couples were the ones who engaged in healthy conflict. They were 10 times more likely in fact, to have a relationship that was happy as opposed to the couples who preferred to ignore or avoid arguments altogether.

According to Maxfield, who is co-authored follow up books to the *Crucial Conversations: Tools for Talking When Stakes are High* books (which were also co-authored by Grenny), the reason these couples are happier was not because arguing was good, but rather because they understand that disagreements are unavoidable and ignoring them is not going to make things any better. The difference was in *how* the couples chose to handle these disagreements. The couples, according to the study conducted, who handled these arguments in a productive way using honesty, love, respect, and by being frank were the ones who experienced a lot more success than the ones who did not.

Grenny and Maxfield also discovered in their study that 4 out of 5 individuals claimed that poor communication was responsible or played a role in the failure of their last relationship. Half the respondents also claimed poor communication was largely responsible for their failed relationship and dissatisfaction which was experienced in the relationship.

Why Productive Conflict Is Good for Your Relationship

Now, you may be wondering how arguments can turn out to be a good thing for your relationship. Here is why handling a conflict in a productive way can be more beneficial for your relationship than you think:

- **Productive Conflict Enables You to Communicate Your Needs -** Arguing provides you with an opportunity to communicate your needs to your partner about what's making you frustrated. Arguments only become unhealthy when you allow negative traits like maliciousness, spitefulness, bitterness, and cruelty get into the mix. What a lot of couples don't realize is that arguments could be handled completely differently and in a mature manner. Use this as an opportunity instead to communicate with your partner and explain to them about why you're feeling the way that you are.

- **Productive Conflict Prevents You From Lashing Out -** You may not like having arguments with your partner, but believe it or not, it is much better than keeping everything bottled up inside. The problem with keeping in all that anger and frustration is that it tends to explode in the most inappropriate moments at times. To prevent this situation is exactly why productive conflicts must be addressed, to keep you or your partner from lashing out in anger later on which could end up being much worse.

- **Productive Conflict Helps You Discover Motives -** According to Dr. Laura VanderDrift, who is an associate professor of psychology based at the Syracuse University in the College of Arts and Sciences, when a couple argues in the right manner, it can actually serve to strengthen their relationship instead of breaking it down. The right manner here being arguing without any form of criticism, contempt or even defensiveness, in other words, engaging in productive conflict. Productive conflict can help you resolve and get to the heart of the matter as to why you're having a conflict of interest, which then helps you discover what your partner's motives may be. Being able to engage in productive conflict will actually help you discover and perhaps learn something new about your partner that you may not have realized prior to this.

- **Productive Conflict Can Help to Save Your Relationship -** A relationship is a lot more likely to break down if you and your partner choose to ignore the serious issues at hand rather than hash it out and try to resolve the problem. If you're always worried about getting into arguments and trying to avoid conflict, what you don't realize is that this creates an even bigger problem because the underlying issue is not being addressed. The so-called "elephants in the room" is the one that is going to be the cause of your relationship falling apart, not productive conflict.

- **Productive Conflict Can Lead to a Change for the Better -** See arguments as a sign that something needs to change. If everything was going well the way that it should, and nothing needed changing, there would be no reason to have an argument, right? Productive conflict can be a good thing because it can push you and your partner towards having a healthy discussion about the changes that need to take place in your relationship for the better and what can you do about it. Good conflict makes you think about what you can do to improve the situation instead of taking a defensive, argumentative stance against it. If you and your partner started viewing productive conflict as an opportunity to make positive changes, your entire perception about arguments will change and you will no longer actively try to avoid conflict any longer.

Chapter 20: Skill #20 – Developing Diplomatic Dialogue Skills

The words that you use during your communication process can have a big impact on the outcome. It isn't just about the tone of voice, but the *words* that you say which is going to have the biggest impact of all on your partner. For example, during a disagreement, you may not be shouting at your partner, but if the words that you utter during those moments are dripping with contempt, harsh and just plain insulting, you those words end up hurting your partner more than if you were actively yelling at them.

This brings us to Skill #20, learning how to develop diplomatic dialogue skills when you communicate with your partner (or anyone else in your life for that matter).

What Does Diplomatic Communication Mean?

Someone who has developed the ability to communicate in a diplomatic manner is someone who has mastered the art of being able to get their messages across the way that they intended and convince the people who are listening to make the changes that they want, *without* causing any harm or damage to the relationship. How are they able to do this so effectively?

For one thing, they don't resort to manipulation to do it, but rather achieve this outcome by communicating with respect, compassion, kindness, and reason. They treat the person with whom they're speaking to as an equal, and they are honest about the things that they say. One might even say that they are *brutally* honest. They don't aim to misrepresent the truth when they communicate, which fosters the element of trust. No matter who they may be speaking to, they always try to interact with the person in a positive manner, making them feel like an important part of the conversation.

Bringing These Diplomatic Communication Techniques into Your Relationship

These are all wonderful traits which you can start bringing into your communication style with your partner and see what an improvement it can make in the way that you talk to each other.

- **Be Mindful of Your Choice of Words -** It is *very important* to be careful about the words that you use. Just one wrong word is all it takes to make a conversation go south and evoke a negative outcome or response. Your choice of words is important because of people's perceptions. Political consultant Frank Luntz even made this aspect a subtitle in his book entitled *Words that Work*, in which he summed it up perfectly by stating that *it is not about what you say, it is about what people hear.* When you're engaged in a productive conflict discussion with your partner, for example, avoid using aggressive words like *you must, you have to, never, always* which foster an element of negativity. Instead, replace those words with more diplomatic language, such as *why don't you consider, I think it might be better, have you ever considered perhaps...* Do you see how just a change of words puts an entirely different spin on the same message? To keep a conversation diplomatic between you and your partner, think about the words you want to use, then re-think about how you could make those words better, then *think yet again* about whether these are the best choice of words to use to achieve the outcome that you want.

- **Be Respectful -** It cannot be stressed enough how important it is to constantly be respectful throughout a conversation if you want to keep the peace. Respect goes a long way, and when you make your partner feel respected like their opinions and ideas are valued, you will see just how different the interaction is going to become. A little bit of an emotional intelligence exercise, here again, is to use empathy and put yourself in their shoes. If they were speaking to you disrespectfully, would you be inclined to just sit there and continue to listen without feeling any kind of negative emotion towards them? Highly unlikely. In fact, that is the quickest way to turn an argument bad, by being disrespectful to your partner when you're having a conversation with them because what you're doing is showing them that you don't care about their feelings at all.

- **Listen and Be Open-Minded -** Communication works both ways, as we've already realized by now. For diplomatic conversations to occur, you're going to have to become an active listener and maintain an open mind. When you don't listen to your partner, you're indirectly telling them that you are not respecting their feelings or their needs - that you don't want to accept their point of view because it may be different from what you want. A key trait of being a diplomatic communicator is to never blurt out the first thing that comes into your head, because that's often how you end up putting your foot in your mouth, especially during a conversation where emotions are running high. Diplomatic communicators actively avoid saying things that they might regret later on, which is why they put a lot of careful thought into their choice of words. Always be a listener first before you become a speaker, and keep an open mind about every conversation, even if you may not necessarily agree with what you hear.

- **Timing is Everything** - Timing matters just as much as what you say. There is a time and a place for everything, and diplomatic communicators know this. If your partner has just come home after having a very hard day at work and they're feeling tense and stressed, would now be a good time to bother them about a task that you've asked them to do but they haven't quite got around to it yet? No, definitely not. Communicating diplomatically means picking the time and the place to hold certain discussions because choosing to bring up something at the wrong time is also going to be hurtful towards your partner, since it shows that you're not considering their needs at that time.

- **No Emotional Reactions** - One thing a diplomatic communicator never does is to react emotionally during a conversation. That's because they know it is impossible to be respectful or tactful during a conversation if your emotions are getting the best of you. This is another diplomatic dialogue skill you need to start practicing with your partner. If you're not feeling calm and composed, then it may not necessarily be the right time to have the conversation that you want.

Chapter 21: Skill #21 - Organizing Romantic Meetings

Almost every relationship begins through some elements of romance, and most couples expect their lovers, co-parents or best friends to continue to be romantic in the relationship. However, sometimes the pressures and demands of life can phase romance out and cause the relationship to evolve and lean towards being more functional than romantic.

Balancing the demands of life and maintaining romance in a relationship can be hard on couples. Throw kids in the equation and the strain becomes worse. Nonetheless, if managed well, relationships can be a source of joy and satisfaction to couples.

Marriage therapist Marcia N. Berger said, *"the art of marriage is really the art of keeping up to date with your partner, of staying on track with your own and each other's life goals as they emerge, exist, and change. It is about supporting each other and staying connected emotionally, intellectually, physically, and spiritually."*

How can couples keep up with all that? By organizing Romantic Meetings.

Benefits of Romantic Meetings

If you and your partner talk daily and wonder why this is important for your relationship, the answer is so that you can intentionally go deeper into discussions that you would most likely brush off when you are pressed for time or do not feel like addressing on the spot.

Sometimes, what we say and what we mean when we

say certain things may not be represented accurately. This can turn into unnecessary misunderstandings that build up emotional stressors over time, especially when we refuse to sit down and discuss it because it was inconvenient or not important at the time. This will eventually reflect through our behavior around each other, affecting both romantic behavior and communication patterns.

A Romantic Meeting can address both functional and emotional needs of a couple. It enables couples to be on the same page and ensures that your relationship steers towards the right direction. This contributes to a more harmonious and orderly home. As you talk things out with your partner during the meeting, you will be able to weed out issues that were not really issues in the first place and make space to discuss real challenges and problems. Removing unnecessary doubt also allows both of you the mental space to be romantic around each other and be intentional about it. Intentional - that is the key to romance.

How to Start Planning Romantic Meetings

Here are some ideas to help you get started on planning for Romantic Meetings:

Set a time

Some couples work best with weekly meetings, while some prefer only once a month. Pick a schedule that suits both of you and adjust the time according to your preferences.

Set the tone

This involves picking a romantic place to dine, or even a familiar place that both of you have fond memories of.

The tone of the meeting is not only set by the location but both of you. Dress the part and bring a positive vibe to the meeting. During the meeting, try to use uplifting and encouraging words instead of criticizing your partner. Please, by all means, flirt and compliment one another as much as you can.

Minimize Distractions

Put your phones away. You have come so far as to set aside time. Make the most of your time together and give each other your full attention. Try to pick a place that both of you are also comfortable to talk and hear each other out. Distractions like sound, television or movement can act as stressors that defeat the purpose of the meeting.

Sit together

Try not to sit across from each other as this can seem confrontational during discussions. Sitting side by side can feel as if both of you are headed in the same direction, together. This gives a sense of unity and the physical closeness can also ignite some romantic feelings.

Write notes

Whatever your partner has to say is important. If you are not the kind of person who pays attention to detail, or has good memory, write them down. You will be talking about to-dos and setting dates for important events. You do not want your partner thinking that what they have to say is unimportant to you.

Own the meeting

The meeting is for both of you. It is important to

understand the goal of meeting together; to build the relationship and rekindle romantic feelings. Give equal time to each other to express thoughts and feelings. If you are usually more verbal and dominant than the other, dial down a little and let your partner speak. Try to work past awkward moments and be true to your aim; better communication, better relationship.

Just the two of you

If it wasn't clear in the beginning, this meeting is for the both of you only. Try not to bring kids or pets that would be a cause for distraction and make you feel more reserved about expressing your thoughts.

Parts of Romantic Meetings

Marcia Berger suggests planning for weekly meetings with your partner that consists of four parts: Appreciation, Chores, Plan for Good Times, and Problems or Challenges.

The Appreciation part of the meeting involves the expression of gratitude towards your partner. These expressions should be specific, 100% positive and touch on behavioral or character traits that you like about your partner. This gives them positive reinforcement and the confidence to continue certain behaviors.

The allocation of chores can be brought up during these meetings as well. Couples can make to-do lists and discuss what else needs to be done. This part of the meeting is meant for couples to work things through together, however, if things get heated and the couple cannot agree on a decision, the discussion is brought to the Problems or Challenges part of the meeting. They can also opt to bring it up in the next Romantic

Meeting.

Thirdly, Berger encourages couples to Plan for Good Times. This involves scheduling date nights or family activities. It gives couples something to look forward to and plan together. This time can also surface common interests or help partners understand each other's likes or dislikes better.

Lastly, discussing Problems or Challenges allows couples to address issues, conflicts or changes in the relationship. This could involve anything from individual insecurities, to who should attend your child's concert or even problems at work. Be determined to make this a safe space for both of you to address concerns without being defensive or judgmental.

Romantic Meetings can look differently for different people, and it is okay to change the format of the meeting to suit both your needs over time. Feel free to improvise and be creative around your meetings so they don't turn into a boring routine.

Chapter 22: The 7-Day Challenge - Workshop to Better Communication

Most couples expect to quickly 'bounce back' to their honeymoon feelings after a Romantic Meeting, but that isn't always the case. Habits, behaviors, communication, and trust is built over time and it varies from one person to another. You probably have people warned you that relationships gradually evolve over time and it takes so much more energy to maintain it, but most of us believe things like that will not happen to us.

The fact that you are reading this means that something has triggered your need or desire to repair or improve your communication with your partner. It also means you are not entirely happy with what both of you have right now. This is absolutely normal for almost every relationship, and it also absolutely okay to feel that way. But before you diagnose or think the worst of your situation, give your partner and yourself a week to figure things out and work towards better communication.

Try this 7-Day Challenge to improve communication with your partner.

Day 1: Reflect and be honest

In the previous chapter, we mentioned the power of being intentional. This first day requires you to be intentional about looking inward and realizing that it takes both time and consistency to make a relationship work. It isn't about what you can do to magically make all communication woes disappear, but how you can work on it.

Be real about the change that you want to see in

yourself. Ask yourself what needs to give, in order for the relationship to be stronger. Being very honest about your why you are going through communication problems and why you behave the way you do will help you be the best version of yourself and inevitably contribute to better communication.

Day 2: Commit to one change

No matter what point you are in your relationship, you are definitely already aware of some of your partner's likes and dislikes. You know their pet peeves and can probably identify what gets on their nerves. Whatever they are, pay attention to them and try your best to change or stop doing certain things that can trigger that. If they like certain things that you do, try to make them more frequent. If there is something that you can do to make them feel better, why not? For example, if you know they enjoy getting little notes of appreciation, drop them more often. If your partner dislikes you leaving the toilet seat down, lift it up when you remember. Little steps like these can go a long way in developing romantic feelings and trust.

Day 3: Say 'Hi' like it's a big deal

Greet your partner like you greet your best friend. Surely, you are happier to have your partner around than when they are away. Make a big deal to acknowledge their presence and express how much they mean to you. We tend to take people we often see for granted, but greeting your partner in a more enthusiastic way can make them feel appreciated and can go a long way in steering your relationship in a different direction. Before you know it, you look forward to this new behavior and enjoy being around each other more.

Day 4: Talk about the bad stuff objectively

You probably won't be able to talk about arguments on the spot, but when both of you have calmed down, take time to hear each other out and be objective about the disagreement. What's valuable about this is that it allows both of you to have a more rational approach to your problems, and this gives both of you the opportunity to resolve the conflict and have closure.

Day 5: Gaze into each other's eyes

No talking and no touching. This seems a little funny, but looking into your partner's eyes builds emotional intimacy. Try this for 10 minutes and gradually increase the length of time. Once you are done, talk about what went through your minds and laugh about it. It will probably feel awkward at first, but doing this daily will help establish an emotional connection and perhaps lead to other kinds of intimacy.

Day 6: Compliment your partner and yourself

Do you find yourself silently adoring your partner? Well, it is worth expressing your admiration. A compliment can be about anything: the way he or she looks, the way they think, how they responded to a problem, or even how they match their clothes. Be genuine about it and try to find something different to complement each other every day. It strengthens your bond and even encourages your partner to repeat the behavior that you like.

We are always too preoccupied with pleasing other people that we tend to forget what we like about ourselves. Make time to recognize the things that you are proud of and give yourself a pat on the back. It is also okay to hug yourself. These are commonly used in therapy to help people who struggle with anxiety and depression. So, while you are complimenting your partner and making them feel good about themselves, give yourself some therapy as well.

Day 7: Ask questions

People change over time and your partner can too. Perhaps both of you are no longer the same people who fell in love years ago. Perhaps it is time to get to know each other again. Ask questions to discover new things about your partner and you'd be surprised to uncover things you have never realized about them. Treating each other like strangers can also ignite excitement and gives you the chance to fall in love with them all over again.

There are no fool proof ways to better communication, and as earlier mentioned, healing and building relationships take time. Some people get better within these 7 days, and some - with the consistent practice of the above - take a little longer. Be patient with each other and remember to be intentional about the things that you say and do.

References:

- https://www.psychologytoday.com/us/blog/fulfillment-any-age/201206/the-12-ties-bind-long-term-relationships

- https://www.heysigmund.com/vulnerability-the-key-to-close-relationships/

- https://www.5lovelanguages.com/

- https://www.thepublicdiscourse.com/2015/12/15983/

- https://www.brides.com/story/body-language-in-relationships

- https://bestlifeonline.com/body-language-tells-every-single-person-should-know/

- https://www.skillsyouneed.com/ips/challenging-conversations.html

- https://www.huffingtonpost.com.au/entry/5-ways-using-your-phone-less-can-improve-your-relationship-and-how-to-do-it_us_55ad0662e4b0caf721b331b7

- https://psycnet.apa.org/record/2014-52280-001

- https://www.pewinternet.org/fact-sheet/mobile/

- https://goodmenproject.com/sex-relationships/approach-difficult-conversations-partner-fiff/

- https://www.yourtango.com/2019322672/daily-horoscopes-today-thursday-march-21-2019-zodiac-signs-astrology

- https://www.mydomainehome.com.au/judgment-bad-for-intimacy-in-relationships

- https://www.cheatsheet.com/health-fitness/how-laughter-can-improve-your-relationship.html/

- https://www.bedsider.org/features/1065-5-reasons-why-laughter-makes-relationships-even-better

- https://www.psychologytoday.com/us/blog/conscious-communication/201703/why-conflict-is-healthy-relationships

- https://www.josephgrenny.com/

- https://hbr.org/search?term=david+maxfield

- http://thecollege.syr.edu/people/faculty/pages/psy/machia-laura.html

- https://www.bustle.com/p/7-ways-arguing-benefits-your-relationship-according-to-experts-8268192

- https://www.prevention.com/sex/g20474958/7-steps-to-improve-your-marriage-in-just-one-week/

- https://www.artofmanliness.com/articles/how-and-why-to-hold-a-weekly-marriage-meeting/

- Ogolsky, B. G., & Bowers, J. R. (2013). A meta-analytic review of relationship maintenance and its correlates. *Journal of Social and Personal Relationships, 30*, 343-367.

Conclusion

Thank for making it through to the end of this book, let's hope it was informative and able to provide you with all of the tools you need to achieve your goals whatever they may be.

For better or worse, in both good and bad times, one constant remain - *couples always need each other.* Every couple goes through hard times, and sometimes even with good communication, you're going to have these challenges. However, good communication can help you overcome these situations much better because you and your partner will now know how to express yourselves openly and freely using all the right techniques and skills.

Finally, if you found this book useful in anyway, a review on Amazon is always appreciated!